Praise for *Hope Unseen*

"Scotty Smiley's story is one all Americans should hear. It will inspire them in tough times and help them through some of the difficult challenges they face in life."

—Senator Bob Dole

"Seldom do stories convey an abandonment of self in giving to others. Captain Scotty Smiley was put to the ultimate test of faith and passed with flying colors, turning what was intended for evil into good. His determination to overcome and to allow God to be honored in the telling of his story is richly conveyed through this book."

—Steven Curtis Chapman,
Grammy Award–winning artist, and Mary Beth Chapman

"When they were classmates at West Point, my son Edward called Scotty Smiley 'the Oak,' because you always knew where he stood. Scotty was an All-American kid—a wrestler and a state champion football player who married his childhood sweetheart, became an elite Army Ranger, and lived by the words of Philippians 4:13, *'I can do all things through Christ who strengthens me.'* Then on April 6, 2005, serving with the army in Mosul, Iraq, Scotty's life was shattered by a car bomb that left him blind. A battle raged within his heart and soul; but when a man's faith is tested and he emerges victorious, the battle is not only won, the enemy is defeated! Living in darkness, Scotty discovered the heart of Philippians 4:13—*'through Christ.'*

In the ensuing years, Scotty has accomplished more than he ever dreamed possible. He currently serves as the army's only active-duty blind officer. He returned to West Point to teach leadership and recently took Command of the U.S. Army Warrior Transition Unit there. I know you will be inspired by the courageous story of Captain Scotty Smiley, and most of all, by his everlasting faith in his Lord and Savior, Jesus Christ.

—Franklin Graham, president & CEO, Samaritan's Purse;
president & CEO, Billy Graham Evangelistic Association

"I love a great story, and the story of Scotty Smiley is not only a great story of a true hero, but this gem is so well written that you will cry, laugh, and cheer as you turn the pages."

—Dave Ramsey, *New York Times* bestselling author

"It's been said, 'The worth of one's character is measured by the trial of adversity.' *Hope Unseen* is a compelling, inspiring, true story about courage, faith, and character revealed. You'll never want to complain about your circumstances again!"

—Lieutenant General R. L. VanAntwerp, U.S. Army

"Scotty Smiley is an American Hero! Scotty and Tiffany have been an inspiration to the Duke Community, to Team USA Basketball, and to me personally. He shared his story with our Olympic Gold Medal—winning basketball team, and now he shares it with all of us to show how character ultimately wins."

—Coach Mike Krzyzewski,
men's college basketball coach of the Duke Blue Devils

"Beyond the extraordinary courage and hope and faith in God that this book brought to life, it was just impossible to put down. Riveting."

—Patrick Lencioni, president of The Table Group;
author of *The Five Dysfunctions of a Team*

HOPE UNSEEN

THE STORY OF THE U.S. ARMY'S FIRST BLIND ACTIVE-DUTY OFFICER

CAPTAIN SCOTTY SMILEY

WITH DOUG CRANDALL

HOWARD BOOKS
A DIVISION OF SIMON & SCHUSTER, INC.
New York • Nashville • London • Toronto • Sydney

The views and accounts expressed in this book are those of the author and do not reflect the official accounts, policy, or position of the U.S. Military Academy, the Department of the Army, the Department of Defense, or the U.S. government.

Howard Books
A Division of Simon & Schuster, Inc.
1230 Avenue of the Americas
New York, NY 10020

First Howard Books hardcover edition September 2010

HOWARD and colophon are trademarks of Simon & Schuster, Inc.

For information about special discounts for bulk purchases, please contact Simon & Schuster Special Sales at 1-866-506-1949 or business@simonandschuster.com.

The Simon & Schuster Speakers Bureau can bring authors to your live event. For more information or to book an event, contact the Simon & Schuster Speakers Bureau at 1-866-248-3049 or visit our website at www.simonspeakers.com.

Designed by Stephanie D. Walker

Manufactured in the United States of America

10 9 8 7 6 5 4 3 2 1

Library of Congress Cataloging-in-Publication Data

Smiley, Scotty.
Hope unseen / Scotty Smiley with Doug Crandall.
p. cm
1. Smiley, Scotty. 2. Christian biography–United States. 3. States–blind–United States–Biography. 4. War wounds–Patients–United States–Biography. 5. Iraq War, 2003—Veterans–United States–Biography. I. Crandall, Doug, 1971- II. Title.
BR1725.S474A3 2010
277.3'083092–dc22
[B]

2010021737

ISBN 978-1-4391-8379-3
ISBN 978-1-4391-8682-4 (ebook)

To My Lord and Savior, Jesus Christ

I CAN DO ALL THINGS THROUGH CHRIST
WHO STRENGTHENS ME.
PHILIPPIANS 4:13

CONTENTS

PREFACE

And now whatever way our stories end
I know you have re-written mine. . . .
Who can say if I've been changed for the better?
But because I knew you I have been changed for good.
Elphaba, in *Wicked*

I first met Scotty Smiley when he visited my leadership class at West Point in the fall of 2006. Not long after that visit, Scotty was offered an opportunity to teach at the United States Military Academy, and our friendship grew as I helped him apply to graduate school. By the summer of 2008 I had left the army and was working as a manager in the Tri-Cities, Washington. Scotty and I hadn't talked in a while. I just knew that he was busy working on his M.B.A at Duke.

My exit from the army ruptured my identity in ways I hadn't anticipated. On a sunny day in August, I hit rock bottom. I was facedown on my bedroom floor in Richland, Washington, my cheeks rubbing the carpet. I didn't want to go to work. I was depressed. I didn't want to feel better—I just wanted to die. It was dark inside me. My wife, Stephanie, had no idea what to do. She just kneeled next to me and pleaded: "Think about Scotty, Doug. Think about Scotty." She left the room and went to pray.

Think about Scotty. Think about all he has been through and how he has emerged. Your problems are comparatively small. Look at the joy he has in his heart.

It's a message that saved my life.

In April of 2007, Scotty had sent me a note: "I would like to thank you with all my heart for your assistance in helping me get accepted to Duke University. I look forward to the opportunities that have opened up for me and know that the Lord is not wasting his time. . . . I wish you were at West Point a few more years so Tiffany and I could hang out with you a little more and *get to know you better.*" It's proven an ironic line.

Though I had left West Point, Scotty and I *did* get to know each other better. Much better. He is now one of my best friends. As it ended up, the Tri-Cities—where I came to work as an operations manager but ended up an author and teacher—is Scotty Smiley's hometown. I'd had no idea of that when I left West Point. We now live ten minutes from his parents. There's no doubt in my mind that God brought us together.

Over pizza last January in Pasco, Washington, Scotty and I started talking about a book. A few months later we were fully engaged in the writing process. On a Tuesday morning in early spring, I was about halfway between Costco's corporate headquarters and Lake Sammamish State Park—right off I-90, at a Tully's Coffee in Issaquah, Washington. I ordered a nonfat vanilla latte, and then I looked around to make sure no one overheard my order. The girl steaming my milk raised her voice above the crackling noise of a skinny metal heating tube and asked me if I had any plans for the day.

"Yes," I said, "I'm flying to Washington, D.C., in a few hours."

"Really?" she inquired. "What's in Washington, D.C.?"

"Well, I left my job to write a book, and I am headed out there to do a few interviews."

Pouring the milk into a cup, she probed further. "What's the book about?"

"It's about this guy named Scotty Smiley. He's an army captain who lost his eyesight in Iraq. He stayed on active duty, climbed Mount Rainier, surfed in Hawaii, earned his M.B.A. at Duke, and is going to teach leadership at West Point."

She stared at me and asked, "Is it a true story?"

Doug Crandall
Richland, Washington
doug@bluerudder.net

PART I

SIGHTED WORLD

Chapter 1

DEPENDENCE DAY

In any and every circumstance I have learned
the secret of being filled and going hungry,
both of having abundance and suffering need.
The apostle Paul, in his letter to the Philippians (chapter 4, verse 12)

"No yellow snow!" was not a suggestion at Mount Rainier's Camp Muir. The climbing guides issued it as an edict. "If you need to go, use the restroom over there—this snow doubles as a source of water at ten thousand feet. None of us wants to go redrinking yesterday's grape Gatorade after it spends the night in your bladder." Easy for them to say. "Over there" was no big deal when you could see. But for a blind guy? I might as well walk to Boise to take a pee; I had zero chance to make it two hundred meters. I had stuck a lot of unwanted things in my mouth during the last eight hundred or so days of darkness, so what was wrong with a tiny taste of lemon snow for a few people who could still see?

The decision quickly became a dilemma. I follow rules. But to pee properly I needed help. I had been superexcited when the guide told our group that we would be waking up at eleven in preparation for the climb to the summit. It was just 9 P.M. Fourteen hours of sleep? Simply awesome. It was smart to allow us rest before we ascended the final four-thousand-plus vertical feet to the fifth-highest point in the continental United States. But my joy was soon turned to frustration: the guide explained that we would be arising at 11 *P.M.* Two hours? I don't mess around with sleep patterns—even if my life now exists in a perpetual nighttime.

By the time I decided that I could no longer hold it, the rest of the climbing team was knocked out. If I woke anyone up, I'd be robbing him of probably half his night's rest. In a departure from my normal worldview, I became a utilitarian. The odds that someone would actually happen upon my urine were extremely low—the Mariners winning the World Series low. Compare those minuscule odds and their minimal impact with the guarantee someone would lose sleep if I shook him awake, and the answer became clear.

At just after 10 P.M., 10,100 feet above Enumclaw and Yakima and Fort Lewis—feet freezing and teeth chattering—I peed in the snow just a few steps behind the tent. Really, the dilemma was less about me stealing anyone's sleep and more about how much I hate—how much I really despise—my childlike dependency on others. With more than two years of blindness under my belt, maybe I should have been used to it, but I wasn't. Being helpless in certain circumstances never gets easy. The pain dulls a bit. But it's a lifelong challenge.

It's difficult to admit, because I like to think of myself as noncompetitive, but the truth is I want to be the best at every endeavor I undertake. Deep down I want to march the fastest, pin the quickest, shoot with the most deadly accuracy, marry the prettiest girl, and climb the highest mountains. That's what happens when you grow up with three brothers and three sisters. You hone your quickness fighting for extra dessert. You build strength and awareness guarding your space in the car. My life growing up was a constant competition, and losing wasn't any fun. So I grew up trying to be the best.

When Micah Clark, the founder of Camp Patriot, invited me on the Mount Rainier climb, I responded by asking him if he knew just exactly who (or what) he was talking to. "I can't see, Micah."

I can't. I still trembled every time those words rolled off my tongue.

I can't. I won't testify with certainty, but I'm pretty sure I never even used those words before the injury. I had won a state football championship—as part of a team of undersized farm boys and wannabes, none of whom went on to play for a Division I school. I graduated from West Point with a decent grade point. I married my beautiful high school sweetheart. I completed Ranger School, and I set my sights on army Special Operations. I feel like I'm a pretty tough guy. I spent my first twenty-four years tackling life head-on with a pretense of invulnerability, pounding life's obstacles into the turf and standing over them, satisfied, with mouth guard in hand. *I can't. Because I can't see Micah.*

"I know you can't see, Scotty. But you can do it."

Micah Clark dreamed up Camp Patriot while fly-fishing in Montana after a three-month stint as a security contractor in Afghanistan. The luxury of a month in solitude—with just his log cabin, his fly rod, and a stream—convinced him that he should do something more for those who had returned from war a little less whole than when they had departed. He believed that outdoor adventures would be therapeutic for wounded vets, so he took a two-hour trip through *Non Profits for Dummies* and launched a dream that continues to shift the paradigm for many of our nation's most giving servants: *I can still be me.*

With Micah's encouragement, I managed to get over "I can't" and agreed to do the climb. Standard climbs up Rainier involve parking a van at about five thousand feet and then a day's walk to double that elevation. There is no real technical climbing involved in the first portion of the journey—not even any snow until a few thousand feet up from the lot. The climactic moment of the first day came when another wounded vet and I crossed Pebble Creek. The creek crossing was nothing more than an exercise in staying dry for people with both eyes or both legs, but it proved a challenge for me. Michael Perry, a writer who joined us on the climb and later published an article in *Backpacker* magazine, described the dynamics: "When they complete the crossing, there are congratulations and smiles all around, but the cheerleading is contained. Everyone is working out the line between encouragement and patronization. The men simply crossed a small creek."

Compared to all the ruck marches I had done as an infantryman, the climb to base camp had not been all that difficult. Foolishly, I announced that to the group, prompting a quick and unfriendly "Shut up, Scotty" from an exhausted fellow climber. "Why don't you try it on one leg?" was his remark. In no way was I reveling in my partner's struggles. To the contrary, I sheepishly apologized to him for my thoughtless comment. But the ease of the movement to base camp—forty-pound backpack and all—had emboldened me.

The next day, two hours into the ascent from Camp Muir, my confidence had vanished, and I was vehemently disagreeing with Micah. I was not sure if I could keep going. Micah Clark—as I remembered him from our years growing up in Pasco, Washington—was an attractive guy, a human rock with a stomach that looked like German hedgerows. When I was a summer lifeguard, he would come to the pool to work out; he was training to become a Navy SEAL.

I'd once been in pretty good shape myself, but Ranger School and my levels of peak fitness were distant memories. Being blind made physical training a struggle. I found it tough to run up hills or to ride a bike. I found the monotony of pounding the pavement without the benefit of passing scenery too much to bear. And so my lungs were not the same as they had once been.

In addition to my burning lungs, both of my calves were ablaze. I wanted to quit. I wanted an hour to hydrate. I was breathing like a chain smoker. I was mentally pummeled. I hoisted the cement pillars that were now my legs up the mountain one deliberate motion at a time. Every single step took Jedi-like concentration, tying my neck and shoulders in taut knots. I had no idea what each succeeding takeoff and landing of my foot would bring. Entertaining the notion that I might make it to the top, I considered the number of steps I still had to take. What was left? Thirty-five hundred feet? The equivalent of eight thousand more stairs? Except that climbing was entirely unlike walking up some steps and a lot more like navigating an angry, oscillating escalator—in the wrong direction and with pieces of metal ready to jab my ankles at any moment.

In my head, I scolded myself. *Why did you agree to do this? Why did you say yes?* How was I going to make it to the top—and then back down again? When we paused for a break, I called out for my escort: "Curtis, I'm not sure I can keep going." I no longer believed I had any chance to summit the mountain.

"We'll see how you feel on the next stop, Scotty."

This guy's not listening to me. I made myself a bit clearer: "Curtis, you don't understand. I don't think I can make it. You guys, um, you guys see these amazing views. You have some motivation to overcome the pain. Me, I don't see anything. I can't see anything. I don't know how much longer I can go."

Curtis handed me a Snickers, some M&M's, and a Propel. "Here you go, Scotty. We'll see how you're doing at the next stop."

I wasn't sure how candy and flavored water were going to fix my fatigued body and my dwindling desire. In fact, I wasn't sure what was going to get me back on my feet. I had been in this spot so many times in the last couple of years. When I woke up from the blast in Iraq and couldn't see a thing, every single step became that much harder. It took determination to get out of bed and just take a shower. It took every ounce of me to learn how to send an e-mail. Daily, I had to make choices to continue on or to sit on the couch with my feet up and listen to the television. When I lost my sight, the linebacker who tackled life head-on—that guy was knocked down. If a blind person tackles life head-on, he runs into things: lampposts, doors, other people. There are lots of things I *can't* do. But there were also lots of things I could still accomplish. I had surfed in Hawaii and skied in Vail. I was about to become a graduate student at Duke University. My life was not as easy as before. Many things were hard. I was learning how to dig deep and fight for things in a new way. And yet, as I sat there on Mount Rainier, I just didn't think I could do *this.*

Two years prior to Rainier, and just three months after losing the use of both of my eyes while fighting the war on terror in Mosul, Iraq, I hit bottom with this battle to persevere. I was struggling to believe that God was still God. I know now that the God who loved me before the injury loved me just as much afterward. The God I hoped in but could not see was the same God I now hoped in despite being able to see nothing at all. But crumpled on a cement slab, in the vicinity of the V.A. Blind Rehabilitation Center in Palo Alto, California, I no longer understood what God wanted from me.

What am I supposed to do with this life? Who am I?

Somewhere along the sidewalk that led to the door of the blind center, my stick had missed a mat. I knew the whole route by heart—had committed it to memory in just a week. Coming out of the gym, I felt around for a metal drainage grate. The grate was maybe twenty feet from the door, just an inch or two to the right of the five-foot-wide cement strip that kept me on course. The xylophone tinging of the grate told me to turn right. Another twenty feet took me to the first black mat—three feet long and five feet wide; the rubber marker told me to take another left. About thirty feet after that turn, I would cross a small driveway—a twenty-foot journey without the benefit of paralleling borders that required me to shoot my own straight arrow to the other side. It was my own personal game of Pin the Tail on the Donkey. Once across the driveway, I would use my stick to again find the sidewalk and resume the "easy" part of my travels.

As best I can remember, I connected all of those dots precisely. Crossing the driveway had the most dramatic impact on my nerves. Parking lots were a blind man's outer space. No up, no down. No left, no right. Just an empty wasteland of concrete that could quickly induce massive disorientation.

Whenever I made it those twenty feet, I breathed a sigh of relief, and on that particular day, I specifically remember exhaling. So it must have been the final waypoint that I missed. My walking stick's next encounter with a black mat meant I would turn right and proceed ten feet until I heard the sound of two automatic doors swinging open. But two minutes after crossing that driveway, I hadn't hit a mat. The stretch to the mat was not really that far—thirty yards and maybe thirty seconds on a normal day. But two minutes? I figure I must have walked a football field. What was the stupid stick for if it couldn't find the mat? I raged against the idea of what I must have looked like with that stick—a spectacle for sure. I was so angry with myself, with the situation, with my pathetic life that I stepped off the sidewalk in defiance. If I had learned one thing in the first week of mobility school, it was "Never leave the sidewalk." *Forget it. I can do this.* I stepped into space and floated toward the moon.

What I didn't know—because Tiffany was carefully picking her battles with me—was that the blue-and-white hockey helmet protecting my brain from a blow to the soft part of my head came with a rainbow-colored chinstrap. I was a triangle-headed man with a stick that shouted, *I can't see,* and I wasn't even aware that it was all made worse by a chinstrap that announced my support for Skittles, trips to Hawaii, or a San Francisco parade. I wouldn't know until weeks later when my friend Adam Rivette visited. Tiffany stood across the room, waving her arms for Adam to be quiet, as Adam asked the obvious question. "Scotty, dude, what's with the rainbow chinstrap?" After Tiffany's sister Michelle hesitantly stuck her toe into the fray and confirmed that Adam wasn't just messing with me, I ripped off the helmet and chucked it across the room.

I had never been to Palo Alto as a sighted person. I had certainly never been to the Blind Center. I had gone toe-to-toe with bullets and bad guys—really bad guys. I had led soldiers in combat. Children at West Point used to look up to me. But sweltering between the mid-July California sun and the radiating pavement—drifting listlessly in that lot—I grew desperate. The blackness, the warmth, and a growing dizziness induced a panic beyond any other that I had ever endured. Before lifting weights at the V.A.'s eighties-era gym, I had neglected to drink any water. I could feel my sweat glands drying up—searching my body in vain for moisture—as I wandered aimlessly, probing for something, anything, that might reestablish my bearings. It was dark. It seemed empty. I felt hopeless.

I fought to stay conscious. Like a bat, I hurled sound waves, shouting "hello" in multiple directions (or what I thought were multiple directions), attuning my ears to any potential echo. But it was well after five. The government workers had all gone home; their punctuality angered me as I clawed at the nothingness for something.

Probably another half an hour went by before I found a curb and its landing. The three-inch increase in elevation was enough to alleviate my fears of being mowed down by a sanitation truck or a spirited teenager fixated on the sounds of hip-hop. I stepped up onto the sidewalk, threw my horrible stick down, and burst into tears. I had lived through a car bomb, narrowly escaped the piercing death of hot bullets, and now I was going to die as a pathetic blind guy in a Silicon Valley parking lot?

As a junior at West Point, I had requested a special inscription on the inside of my class ring. The woman taking my order had looked up and asked me with a surprised smile who "Phil" was. I chuckled inside and then explained that Phil was not a person but a book of the Bible. Tucked up next to the skin on the fourth appendage of my right hand is a small reminder that reads *Phil 4:13*—a reference to the verse from Philippians "I can do all things through Christ who gives me strength." I once believed *I* could do anything—so much so that I went out of my way to carve it into the ring I wear on my finger. But in the emptiness of that parking lot, I quickly understood that I could do almost nothing at all, and I wondered if God even wanted to help me. I goaded God to tell me how I was supposed to take care of my family if I couldn't even walk back from the gym.

God, what do you want from me? Why am I here? How am I supposed to wake up every day and live like this?

"Scotty. Get up. Let's go," ordered Curtis in the most polite way possible. I propped up my body with my axe, tried to shake off the massive fatigue, and trudged on—step by step—up Mount Rainier. I was living out that choice again—the choice to keep going. *I can do all things through Christ. . . .* I had always wanted to climb this mountain, ever since I'd seen it as a kid while driving west toward Seattle from my home in the eastern part of Washington. The vantage of Rainier from Fort Lewis, where I had been stationed since leaving West Point, charmed me on every single one of the Pacific Northwest's clear days. Whether from the living room of the corps commander's home or from the drive-thru at Burger King, Mount Rainier was Fort Lewis's Mona Lisa. There was no escaping its gaze. I had last looked upon Rainier the day I left for Iraq. I stood on the airfield and saluted the snowy peak before climbing on an airplane.

When I finally agreed to do the climb, I thought that maybe if I made it to the crest of that enormous snowcapped rock, I could be the best again—that someone ordering a Whopper Jr. and fries would look up and see me through their binoculars. I would wave back. "I'm blind, but I'm on top of Mount Rainier." Those were nice thoughts—they kept my heart warm and my pride intact before the onset of my cramping legs and the melting of my mental fortitude. Now, though, hope was becoming a memory. Much of the climb was in the mind, and as I mentioned before, my brain had all but given up on the prospect of actually scaling the summit—probably about a Space Needle ago.

Nonetheless, I had eaten the Snickers, downed the M&M's, and sucked in some Propel. Whether it was the peanuts and caramel or the prayer, somehow my strength returned. The cement around my legs cracked and crumbled to the ground. Unbelievably, my newfound energy carried me up the mountain for the next several hours. I listened to Curtis, followed his steps, and trusted he would not lead me astray. The trust reduced the tension that had hindered me to that point. While the climb remained tedious and painful, I began to believe again.

The point of no return came during the crossing of a narrow ice bridge. It was a truly perilous portion of the climb for a blind person. The fragile nature of the bridge restricted its use to only one passenger at a time. My inability to see actually helped me overcome my fear of heights. The sight of the two-thousand-foot crevasse waiting below surely would have paralyzed me on the near side of the frozen balance beam. But unable to process my fear visually, I looped myself onto the safety line and picked up the sound of Curtis's confident voice. "Put one foot in front of the other, Scotty. One foot in front . . . careful . . . easy . . . one foot in front of the other. Step in your steps." Climbers do not die on Rainier at the rate that Everest claims lives, but many of those who have perished scaling Washington State's largest mountain reportedly surrendered to the claws of just such a crevasse.

I could tell by Curtis's careful tone that we were in a dangerous spot. Earlier, Micah Clark had dropped his axe while moving along the ice bridge. It spiraled across the slick surface and clinked and clanked a few times before falling into the bowels of the mountain. The climbers in his group had steadied their ears to ascertain the sound of the axe hitting bottom. They never heard a thing.

"One foot in front of the other. That's good, Scotty."

Twelve hours after we had begun our final stretch of the journey, I placed my size eleven boots on the 14,410th foot of Mount Rainier. I turned and told a video camera: "I love you, Tiffany." After the shout-out to my wife, I stood up straight and painted a mental picture of my surroundings. My heart swelled with confidence. I knew exactly where I stood. I'd looked up at the top of the mountain so many times before. At that moment, I was the biggest thing up there. I made it. I really did. I couldn't see a thing. But Micah was right. I made it.

I was not the first blind person to climb Rainier—five people without sight did it together in 1981. There had probably been others in the twenty-six years since. Nor is Washington State's highest peak the crowning achievement of sightless climbers. A blind Erik Weihenmayer summited Everest in 2001. Rainier is not even that big a mountain, but it felt like an unreachable peak at many moments during the climb. Somehow I had made the choice to keep going, and others had come alongside to make persevering possible. We are dependent on God and dependent on one another. I just couldn't see it until I was blind. Sight notwithstanding, in some way, every day is dependence day.

I had other things to do that day. A month earlier, I had oddly been named the 2007 *Army Times* Soldier of the Year. Before I climbed Rainier—which I'd done now; I'd climbed all the way up it—my story had been one example of an entirely new way of imagining our wounded warriors. All kinds of soldiers just like me had shifted themselves from people to be pitied and thanked to servants who had more to give. So to represent others like me, I should have been en route to Washington, D.C., for the Soldier of the Year festivities. Tiffany, not all that happy about my sudden jones for sightless mountain climbing, nonetheless volunteered to stand in for me on the first day of events in D.C. I would arrive just in time for the actual ceremony.

Hearing a plane soar just above my head, I allowed myself to believe that maybe Tiffany, on her way to the nation's capital holding baby Grady, looked down on me with pride from a window of that jet. I waved—just in case—and thanked her for everything she had done to get me to this point.

Chapter 2

SUMMER FRECKLES

I left Washington 13 October 2004 with sorrow, fear,
and anticipation of the upcoming year. Sorrow for leaving the
most beautiful woman in the world and my best friend,
Tiffany, for a year; fear for the unknown
and what God had in store for my platoon and marriage.
My first journal entry, 19 October 2004

Although I wasn't able to see the YouTube video, just the sounds and description of it haunt me. Clothed in black, three members of the Iraqi militant group Ansar Al-Sunna (an infamously brutal affiliate of al-Qaeda in Iraq) sat side by side in front of a video camera. The man in the center read rhythmically from a piece of paper that he held with both hands. Apparently, he folded and unfolded the script as he traversed the text. I'm not sure how he saw the words—his head was covered with a black hood. His cadence, in fact, underscored a rehearsed message. The Arabic words were foreign and unintelligible to me, and the reader used a malicious tone, a weapon intended to strike fear in the heart.

The two men flanking the reader held machine guns on their laps. Both weapons pointed toward the ceiling. The man to the right wore an armored vest, and through a slit in his hood, an eyeball glimmered.

The vest was army green. But everything else—the men's clothing, the backdrop—was black. It all seemed evil. The sounds told me that much.

In the bottom right corner of the video, a date stamp read *20 12 2004.* It was my first wedding anniversary.

The reader finished his recitation, and the video suddenly went silent. The camera zoomed to a schematic of several buildings. Using a hunting knife—probably six inches long and an inch wide—as a pointer, one of the men worked through a plan. He identified key spots on the map, and though he never pointed directly to it, in the top right corner was what looked like a large tent. I am told that it was the most distinguishable feature on the sketch.

The video switched back to the original room. Two of the men were no longer sitting. The man in the middle and the man with the armored vest embraced in front of the camera, patting each other on the back in the way that men do. For an instant, their affection seemed, I am told, to brighten the sinister scene. The third man was sitting with his hands on his lap and his weapon in front. He rose and awkwardly embraced the man with the armored vest. Then the video transitioned to the next day.

I did not get the chance to call Tiffany on our first anniversary—not according to the calendar in Iraq at least. But just before lunchtime in Mosul (and a few hours after midnight in Pasco, Washington), I dialed Tiffany's cell phone number and startled her awake at her parents' house. I had waited in line for an hour to make this call, knowing that Tiff would want to share some time with me—even if I was a day late and could only find a moment in the middle of her night.

Once she rubbed her eyes open and adjusted her senses to the volume of her own voice, it was a great conversation. Most of our conversations are. We are best friends. That night, we reminisced about our wedding, honeymoon, and my abrupt departure for Ranger School. In our first year of marriage, we had spent only a handful of months together. I promised that when I returned, we would do a second honeymoon with walks on the beach, late night conversations, and hours of uninterrupted companionship.

After thirty minutes were up, I said good-bye. "I'm going to head to lunch," I told my wife with regret. Tiffany cherished these moments, even at 3 A.M. even if only for half an hour, and saying good-bye always left her with a sense of emptiness. I know Tiffany tried not to let me sense the pain she felt, but I could feel it anyway.

I loved the phone calls too. My dreams in Iraq were clearer than any I'd had in my own bed. In sleep, I could see Tiffany's slender neck; I would hold her close and brush my cheek with her hair. When I woke up, I would live in that moment for as long as I could. But aside from my dreams, these phone calls were all I had of her. When I could not hear Tiffany's voice or look at her picture, she would fade from memory in a painful way.

Tiffany is beautiful. She is not the normal kind of beautiful, but drop-dead beautiful. The kind of gorgeous that makes it unclear whether Tiffany should be sitting in the chair across the living room from me or sitting next to the chair, in the magazine rack . . . on the cover of *Glamour.* I loved Tiffany's freckles—especially in the summer. She also has a wonderful smile—not just her teeth and mouth, but the way her eyes grin and her head tilts slightly as her smile turns to laughter. The freckles, the teeth, and the smiling eyes all made me do a double take every time I saw her. Now, I know it's my wife I'm bragging about, but she is really that special—at least in my eyes (or in my memories).

My emotional affection barely outpaces my physical desire for Tiff. On this, the day after our paper anniversary, I relived our wedding night: the best night of my life. Friends sometime hassle me, suggesting we had the shortest wedding reception on record, stopping for a dance, cake, and a couple of pictures en route to the hotel. "It was like, where did they go?" A rhetorical question, I guess. We had waited five years.

From the time I was a teenager, I have loved this woman with every ounce of me. She is a godly woman. I'm blessed to be married to her. Not lucky, but blessed. I met my gorgeous best friend when she was Tiffany Elliott—a cute-as-can-be sixth-grader at McLoughlin Middle School. She had a crush on me. She even went home and told her mom: "This Scott Smiley—I could like him." But I didn't like girls. Not yet. At McLoughlin's eighth-grade graduation ceremony, Tiffany tried again. I won a bunch of middle school awards that made me pretty proud of myself at the time. Tiffany reminded her mom that *I* was the guy—the one she had been chasing. Karen Elliott, who was as much sister to her daughter as she was mother, bumped into my mom. "My daughter really likes your son," Karen hinted to Mom.

"I'm sorry," my mom retorted, "but Scotty doesn't like girls." Not yet. Persistent to only a point, Tiffany took her looks and focused on older guys for a while.

Yet finally came. During the summer before our junior year, I built up my courage and called Tiffany. I asked her to coffee. I'm not sure why coffee specifically. We were only sixteen, for goodness' sake. But coffee was better than bowling. It seemed like the thing to do.

On a Sunday night in midsummer, I disappeared down the hallway to make a phone call while the rest of my six siblings waited in the family room for the result. Nervous as all get-out, I dialed; I hung up. And then I dialed. And then I hung up. And then I dialed and let it ring until the ringing ceased and a tender voice replaced it. And when I emerged with bad news—that Tiffany didn't want to grab a cup of coffee—all of the Smileys heckled me in concert. Tiffany, it seemed, had basketball practice. It was a weird excuse—basketball practice on a Sunday night in July. The butterflies in my stomach vanished. *She lied to me,* I thought, as my dad chuckled in the background. *Basketball practice. Whatever.*

It wasn't until a year later that I first noticed the freckles. It was a scorching summer day before my senior year. Tiffany and a friend were stuck in the middle of the Columbia River—east of where I-182 crosses over from Richland to Pasco in the Tri-Cities, Washington, a community of just over two hundred thousand, about three hours east of Seattle. A grumpy old boat had broken down. Two teenage girls, bikini-clad, tan, and stranded, called out for help. My brother Stephen and I spotted them—helpless—and coasted in to the scent of burning oil and dead engine. Whether it was the more attractive smell of Hawaiian Tropic or my irresistible good looks, it took Tiffany about one-point-three seconds to jump in with us. I think her friend must have come too, but I don't really remember.

The next night, we were at the movies: *Five Days and Four Nights,* or *Four Days and Five Nights*—something like that. I drove us in my dad's cherry red 1965 Mustang, a car my three younger sisters would eventually run into the ground. Tiffany didn't really care about the car or its vinyl seats. And as we remember it, she didn't really say much on that first date. I guess I did all the talking. "Literally, all the talking," claims Tiffany. I talk a lot when I am nervous. And I was nervous. From traffic light to traffic light, I chattered in bursts.

At the end of our date, I asked Tiffany if I could give her a kiss. Though the request came half from chivalry and half from postpubescence, Tiffany nonetheless appreciated it and acquiesced. It was an awkward kiss, sort of twisted, and on the side of her face. "Half lip and half cheek," as Tiffany recalls. Really, the date would have been better without it. "Why did you do that?" she asks me every couple of years. I guess I figured it would probably be my last chance. It wasn't.

We broke up once during my freshman year at West Point. Tiffany, while a pre-nursing student at Columbia Basin College, decided she should see "other people" and suggested, even if halfheartedly, that I do the same. She dabbled, but didn't find what she was looking for. It wasn't really a fair offer on Tiffany's part. West Point was 85 percent male. I had fewer chances to dabble. But lucky for me, I was the only needle in Tiffany's haystack.

Tiffany enjoyed my disposition and goofiness; and she tells me she really appreciated my faith. As a guy, I thought her admiration would be about my skills as a linebacker, our state football championship, or my waterskiing ability. Maybe she would like me because I was on my way to West Point. Her love is about none of that—something that would prove abundantly true when I lost my eyes.

The time stamp in the bottom right corner of the video now read *21 12 2004; 12:03:20.* The camera no longer saw three men in a room but was looking at an empty sky with trees in the foreground. A loudspeaker blared a halting chant. In the distance, beyond the trees and the chanting, the camera spotted the outline of a white tent. Just a few minutes earlier, I had eaten lunch in that tent—the mess tent at Forward Operating Base (FOB) Marez in Mosul, Iraq, about 250 miles northwest of Baghdad in the province of Nineveh. I spent most of my lunch losing myself in the phone conversation I'd just had with Tiffany. The food tasted okay; the macaroni and cheese needed some salt. But eating was merely a necessity at this point. Food filled only my physiological emptiness.

For the last part of my meal, I shared the tent—a distant cousin of the hasty shelters found at trade shows or county fairs—with my company commander, Captain Bill Jacobsen. "Captain J.," thirty-one years old, was six feet five inches tall, a BYU graduate, Eagle Scout, husband, and loving father of four. At lunch, Captain J. sat next to Sergeant Pena, the company sniper, and across from Lieutenant Coughlin, the Alpha Company executive officer, Captain J.'s second in command.

I departed the dining facility as Lieutenant Dave Webb entered. Dave was one of three friends whom I considered my best buddies back at West Point. He is a sharp-looking guy with a head of dark black hair. He is always in shape. He can walk around Hawaii with his shirt off and women will thank him. In Mosul, we read the Bible and prayed together, talked about our wives, and dreamed about going home. But as we crossed paths at the mess tent, Dave just wanted me to join him for lunch. He was not concerned that I had already eaten; he wanted my companionship, even if only for a bit.

I thought through Dave's request but knew I needed to get back and prepare for an upcoming mission. Engaged in our trivial conversation, neither one of us noticed Ahmed Said Ahmed al-Ghamdi; at some point, he must have passed behind us and entered the tent.

There was nothing to notice really. We had no idea who he was. Ahmed, a twenty-year-old Saudi medical student, had been working at FOB Marez for close to two months. He wore a standard Iraqi security uniform and was one of many security officers who would eat there each day.

Dave said good-bye to me, made his way through the sandwich line, and found a seat in the far corner of the dining facility as Ahmed looked for a location of tactical adequacy, properly situated within range of the densest crowd of eaters. After some wandering, he positioned himself in the chow line among a mass of people, a few feet diagonally from one of the lunch tables. Under his Iraqi uniform, Ahmed carried a pack full of death. In his hand, he held a detonator.

CHAPTER 3

NO NEWS

Endow us with courage that is born of loyalty to all that is noble and worthy, that scorns to compromise with vice and injustice and knows no fear when truth and right are in jeopardy. . . . Help us to maintain the honor of the Corps untarnished and unsullied and to show forth in our lives the ideals of West Point in doing our duty to Thee and to our Country.

The Cadet Prayer

At 12:03:58 Ahmed Said Ahmed al-Ghamdi blew himself up.

On the way back to my trailer—about a half mile from the mess hall—I heard an explosion but thought it was just another artillery episode. After two months in Iraq, I learned mortar attacks were about as eventful as rain in Seattle, if not more commonplace. The single blast puzzled me—the claps of man-made thunder usually came in bunches—but it did not concern me enough to occupy my thoughts for more than a moment. I continued back to my trailer—my temporary home—and began my combat preparations.

Later I learned that it took only one blast to throw the mess tent into disarray—to level the sort of destruction that Ahmed Said Ahmed al-Ghamdi had given his life to inflict. The concussion knocked my friend Dave Webb from his chair, but his seat was far enough from Ahmed to spare him an injection of flying shrapnel and ball bearings.

Along with a herd of others, he rushed out of the tent and took cover in the nearby bunkers—standard operating procedure for reaction to a rocket attack.

At the table closest to Ahmed Said's chosen point of detonation, Sergeant Pena and Lieutenant Coughlin were not sure what had happened to Captain J. Our commander's eyes began to swell and roll back toward his brow, and then his head fell forward onto the table. Screams, debris, smoke, and chaos surrounded Pena and Coughlin, but they were entirely focused on the captain. "Sir," Pena yelled. "Sir, wake up!" Captain Jacobsen did not move. He wasn't breathing. His heart had stopped.

Sergeant Pena and Lieutenant Coughlin moved Captain Jacobsen to the floor and began CPR. Pena propped the captain's head up, opened his mouth, and attempted to blow life into his body. When the breaths were done, Sergeant Pena located the sternum, inched down, and attempted to pump blood through the arteries of his commander. Life flickered on and off like a streetlamp, but Sergeant Pena couldn't get it to hold.

This same scene repeated itself in multiple spots around the FOB Marez mess tent. Thirteen U.S. soldiers and nine others died that day. A half mile away, a handheld video camera recorded a small boom and a puff of smoke. At 12:04:10, the camera turned off.

A hasty crew carried Captain Jacobsen toward a vehicle. FOB Marez was not equipped to handle this sort of casualty, so medics rushed Captain J. to the next base over.

Within minutes, a soldier knocked furiously on my door. I opened it to see a young man with burnt hair and scrapes on his leg. There was an explosion in the mess hall, the singed messenger announced. "It was big." The soldier was yelling, not even able to hear himself talk because of what the enormous boom had done to his ears. When I arrived outside the chow tent, it looked like a disheveled bazaar. Army vehicles swarmed the perimeter, protecting against follow-up tremors. I saw stretchers all around and bloody bandages strewn along the ground. I tried to get inside to help, but a guard had been posted at the mess hall's entry, prohibiting anyone from going inside. I peered into the tent and caught a glimpse of a twenty-foot slice of the sky through a hole in the ceiling. Tables and chairs were scattered everywhere. People guessed that a rocket had come through the top, or that someone had hidden a bomb. But no one knew exactly what had happened. Days later, Ansar al-Sunna—the al-Qaeda affiliate—claimed responsibility for the bombing.

Tiffany awoke at 6:30 A.M. to make it to the clinic by 7:30. With a twelve-hour nursing shift ahead, she hurried to check her e-mail before departure. Tiff loved when my name filled her inbox, even if she had just talked to me on the phone. She anticipated the e-mails so much that she patiently endured the humming and cranking of the dial-up Internet at her parents' house, where she was staying for the duration of my deployment.

The computer stopped spewing out buzzing noises as Yahoo worked its way onto the screen. Before Tiffany could put her finger to the mouse, headlines flashed with news of a Mosul mess hall bombing at lunchtime—with dozens of casualties and a mounting death toll. Tiffany froze in her chair, gripping the armrests, closing her eyes, and hoping I was still alive. She remembered my words on the phone: "I'm going to head to lunch . . ."

Fourteen hours would pass without any information about me.

Dave Webb's family received a short e-mail telling them that he and a few others were okay; there was no mention of my whereabouts or condition. The phones had all been shut off for security reasons. I was occupied with the response to the attack and unable to get to e-mail. So Tiffany waited in silence. She zombied her way through a day checking blood pressures, feigning normalcy, fighting back tears, and taking deep breaths as coworkers inquired about my well-being. Friends and family tried to assure her that "no news was good news." But really, no news was just no news.

By the time Tiffany headed home at eight-thirty, it was dark. The isolation of the car and the quietness of the drive calmed her to some degree. God was in control—that was a lesson Tiffany understood in her head, but one that both of us would learn with our hearts in the coming months and years.

At home she went straight to the computer. She desperately hoped to have a message about my safety. In fact, Tiffany received one e-mail. Riikka Jacobsen—the wife of Captain Jacobsen—had written to all of the Alpha Company family members: "No word yet. We are still hoping and praying." The disappointment of the message was muted only a bit by the knowledge that Riikka, a caring mother and wife with a sweet Finnish accent, shared a seat in this same turbulent boat.

As Tiffany processed the e-mail, two headlights made their way down my in-laws' driveway. When she noticed the car, Tiffany panicked and cried out: "No, Lord! Please, no!" She begged God that these casualty assistance officers—if that's who they were—would take their horrible news elsewhere. She did not want anyone to thank her for my sacrifice. The inevitability of the moment hit her as the lights continued up the driveway toward the house, and then around to the side, by the garage.

Tiffany clung to her chair. If she didn't move, she didn't have to lose me. Tears filled her eyes. Her heart pounded. The day before had been our first anniversary. After five years of waiting—four of them spent three thousand miles apart—Tiffany and I had finally married each other. Now, the day after our first anniversary, I was gone? She couldn't bring herself to ask, *Why me?* Tiffany knew there were others suffering as well. She knew this was what I had signed up to do. She knew I believed in it, loved it even. She believed it in it too. But not right now.

Nearly lost in her anguish, Tiffany suddenly realized the doorbell had not chimed. She looked out a window to her right and saw the red glow of taillights leaving the driveway. Later, she learned a friend had dropped off some electrical supplies for Mr. Elliott. No news was good news.

I have three brothers and three sisters. Neal, Stephen, and I are the oldest. Then come the three sisters—Mary Lynn, Krista, and Kathleen—followed by Nick, the youngest. All seven of us children are the offspring of two loving parents—Rick and Mary Ann. Our Smiley team would joyfully share a single room at a Motel 6 if necessary and would even invite Mom and Dad to come inside. Chances are we would watch *Wheel of Fortune* and play Hearts while eating pizza. It all sounds kind of over-the-top sappy, I am sure. But I grew up in a great family, and I love every one of them.

My brother Neal gets most of the credit for the military idea. He became enamored with West Point while listening to the Christmas-day stories of Michael Foley. Michael was a family friend—a "cousin"—and a 1985 graduate of the United States Military Academy.

When he visited, he would sit on the couch and talk of the beauty of the academy. There were harrowing granite buildings that rose above a grassy plain. To the north, a skyscraping obelisk known as Battle Monument towered above a picturesque vantage called Trophy Point.

Trophy Point and its monument looked north to where the Hudson River cut between a pair of tree-adorned slopes and ran past Newburgh to the left. New Windsor, New York, just south of Newburgh, was the location of George Washington's final encampment and the home of the Purple Heart Hall of Fame. On a bright day, as the sun glistened off the Hudson, cadets marched across the grassy plain and the West Point Band belted out songs from our nation's history. Immortalized in bronze, Eisenhower, MacArthur, and Patton stared down approvingly.

Michael told one story from his early army days that captivated us. At Ranger School, a splinter made its way into his eye. He was evacuated to the hospital and spent several hours in the waiting room. He had some change in his pocket and so visited the vending machine. Standing in front of a collection of candy and snacks—starving and with a pirate patch to protect his wound—Michael endured an epic struggle to decide between Three Musketeers and Snickers. Ranger School had driven him to such severe hunger that the candy bar decision ranked as one of the most difficult of his life. We thought our cousin and his legendary hunger were cool. The stories were exciting. In our mind's eye, we too would wear uniforms, march on the plain at West Point, graduate, starve at Ranger School, and suffer injury. We would launch our bodies from airplanes, camouflage our torsos with tree branches, crawl through the mud, and lob grenades at those who threatened freedom.

Neal was so sure of his destiny that West Point was his only plan.

He put pencil to no other college applications, lined up no jobs at Wal-Mart, and considered no alternatives. On an icy winter's day in early 1996, Neal traveled an hour west to Yakima to interview with a West Point admissions panel assembled by Congressman Doc Hastings. Neal was nothing if not confident. My older brother had a head like a poodle and a chest like a Disney character. Mom has called him "kind of" cocky, but the "kind of" qualifier clearly stems from a mother's love. There was no "kind of."

Peering at him from behind a folding table, the panelists could not quite understand why Neal had applied only to West Point—why someone who thought he had the intelligence to succeed at the United States Military Academy would not have the wisdom to formulate a backup plan. Slamming down a gavel of words that resonated in his ears, a member of the panel told my brother that he "was not West Point material."

But Smileys don't quit. Neal pressed on and with the help of Michael Foley took his cause to Senator Slade Gorton. The West Point application process is unique. A candidate has to win the approval of two different assessors: his or her congressman or senator, to gain a nomination, and then West Point itself. Members of Congress typically submit ten names for each opening in their district, and then West Point decides whom to admit. West Point, it seemed, wanted Neal. The admissions office saw him as prototypical army officer material. With the academy's stamp of approval, my brother gained a nomination from Senator Slade Gorton. He entered West Point that same summer, the first Smiley in recent memory to don a military uniform.

Because of Michael Foley and Neal, I chose to apply to West Point as well. In contrast to Neal, on the day of my own interview I was extremely nervous. As I sat rehearsing responses in my head, a uniformed teenager came through a door and flashed a confident smile in my direction. The competition wore medals on his chest that he had earned as a member of a local Junior ROTC organization. He had a tight haircut, an upright posture, and he already looked the part of a West Point graduate. My head swiveled to watch him walk out the door, my West Point aspirations seemingly heading out with him.

But some of the fortune that escaped Neal shined its light on me. Later that day, I was to play in the Washington State 4A football playoffs. The panelists at my interview wanted to know about the game. I talked sports, leadership, teamwork, and strong side blitzes for the better part of twenty minutes. After that they asked me some other stuff. I don't remember what I said, and I probably did not make much sense; but I did well enough to gain admission. I ended up choosing West Point. I really wanted to lead soldiers.

Neal graduated from West Point three years ahead of me, but by the luck of the draw, I ended up in Iraq first—the first one to eat lunch in an exploding mess hall. Wondering about my safety on the day of the Mosul bombing, Neal dialed up a friend at Fort Lewis to collect some information. With slick talking and persistence, he pried away all he needed to know: the battalion's killed-in-action (KIA) list did not include my name. Neal delivered the good news to Tiffany at 10 P.M: I was okay.

Tiffany laid her head down on her pillow that night, thankful I was alive. On days like this one, the support of friends and family became crucial. Therese Van Antwerp, Tanya Webb, and Riikka Jacobsen were all women on whom Tiffany depended. With their husbands away, the women would get together for dinner and share sisterhood, stories, and emotions.

The bond that Tiffany felt with Riikka Jacobsen made the next morning one of immense pain. Friends and family showered Tiffany with messages of relief that I had escaped harm. But a few hundred miles west, across the Cascade Mountains, Riikka was receiving the news that Tiffany and so many others had feared. Riikka learned what those of us at FOB Marez had known for nearly a day: her husband was not okay. Captain Bill Jacobsen had been the first—and senior ranking—soldier declared dead at the hands of Ahmed Said Ahmed al-Ghamdi.

December 21, 2004, was Riikka and Bill Jacobsen's ninth wedding anniversary.

Chapter 4

AT SIX

I waited patiently for the Lord;
And he inclined to me and heard my cry.
He brought me up out of the pit of destruction,
out of the miry clay,
And He set my feet upon a rock, making my footsteps firm.
He put a new song in my mouth, a song of praise to our God.
King David (Psalm 40, the inspiration for the song "40" by U2)

As best I can remember, I'm a pretty good-looking guy. I have dark brown hair with bright blue prosthetic eyes. My prominent nose juts out above my slightly crooked smile. I was born with that smile (a nurse at Walter Reed would later think it was a result of my injury) and have been ridiculed for it throughout my life. If it wasn't my smile kids were making fun of, then it was my clothes. Each summer, my mom would take a pair of orange-handled scissors and turn my Levi's into shorts. Other kids always had new stuff to wear, but with seven of us, Mom had to improvise.

As a kid, I learned pretty quickly not even to attempt to go out and play in the mornings without having read my Bible. My mom would spot me inching toward the front door and ask, "Scott Michael Smiley, have you read your Bible yet today?" I would just lower my head, put myself in reverse, and go back into my room. My mom's disciplined approach to our Bible study also applied to the kind of language we used in our home and the television shows we were allowed to watch. We attended church every Sunday at Faith Assembly in Pasco. I carried similar practices into my adult life, and I think my external displays of faith—the Bible reading, clean mouth, church attendance—are part of the reason my friends at West Point called me "the Oak." I tried not to sway from my principles.

Edward Graham, Dave Webb, Adam Rivette, and I were a foursome at West Point with distinct roles. All four of us taught local children in Sunday School. On the only day that guaranteed sleep past six-thirty (we often had parades, military training, or physics exams on Saturday mornings), we sacrificed Sunday slumber to sing songs, referee games of Heads-Up Seven-Up, serve as human climbing walls, and share a little bit of Jesus. We received a lot more than we gave. It was great to be around the kids.

Dave, who would be with me later in Iraq and would feel the blast of that exploding mess hall, was the de facto leader of our group, at least from a logistical standpoint. If we headed to New York City for a three-day weekend, then Dave decided what time to jump on the Metro North at the Garrison train station, which Manhattan hotel room we could get at the lowest cost, and what time we needed to start the trek back to West Point to make it in time for accountability formation. As most leaders do, Dave took the abuse. If the hotel room smelled of wet dog, if the fries were too salty, or if the cab cost too much, it was Dave's fault. We saw him as the CEO—a "businessman" who not only taught Sunday school but served as the cadet superintendent, responsible for everything that happened on Sunday mornings. The eldest child of a White House Fellow and Harvard Business School graduate, Dave possessed a keen ability to jump in and take over. He was the cadet in charge of Officers' Christian Fellowship and an active member of the West Point parachute team. Looking back, Dave says that he should have poured a little more effort into his academic endeavors, but he did well enough to finish just a spot behind me—and I studied all the time.

Adam Rivette was the wild card. Son of a career army officer and a Venezuelan mother, Adam bounced left and right to avoid the shadow of his older brother Daniel, who graduated from West Point in 2001. He never did anything *really* wrong, but Adam definitely had some rebel in him. Adam is a scrawny six feet. His kneecaps are wider than his thighs. He has dark hair and tans the way every one of us fair-skinned people wishes we could. Adam is the spitting image of the little East Indian character in *The Jungle Book,* so we called him Mowgli.

The cadet punishment for infractions—minor and major—is to put on full dress uniform and march back and forth between the barracks for hours at a time. Adam walked over one hundred hours on the area, earning the title "Century Man." Most cadets combine an egregious mistake (drinking in the barracks or leaving post without authorization) with a couple of smaller errors to reach the one-hundred-hour threshold. Drinking in his room can quickly vault a cadet to eighty hours, in which case he just needs to miss a couple of classes or return late on a weekend to reach the century mark. Adam Rivette earned over one hundred hours in an entirely unique way: crossing the hall to the bathroom in only his boxers, forgetting to wear his name tag to class, and turning in his assignments late. He nickel-and-dimed his way into cadet penal history—quite an impressive feat.

Edward Graham and I became solid friends during our first year at West Point. We toiled as opponents in the 197-pound weight class on the Army Wrestling Team. Back then, I used to dominate him.

Edward says I didn't really beat him with skill; it's just that I used to head-butt him all the time. He would whine that it was only practice and there was no reason for me to beat him to death with my head. Whatever his excuse, I was better. At the outset of sophomore year, I left the wrestling team to focus on academics and military endeavors, but I am proud of having been able to go toe-to-toe with Edward. He is a six-foot-four muscular beast with a long torso and legs that are disproportionately short. I wouldn't grapple with him today, even if I could see.

Even though I'd known him basically since I got to West Point, Edward was the last one to join our group of friends. As he became comfortable with us, Edward played bully. He became the indignant big brother who believed, deep down, that none of us should mess with his considerable mental aptitude or dominating physique. This despite the fact that his grades were the lowest and I had regularly pummeled him on the wrestling mat. "You know I'm right," Edward would say as he insisted that the Garden State Parkway was the best route to the Meadowlands. "Whatever," we would respond with our eyes as we shot looks across the car and headed down the New Jersey Turnpike. Such disrespect resulted in Edward grabbing Adam and putting him in a headlock. Edward was arrogant in the best possible way.

During the winter of senior year, Edward's father, Franklin Graham, hosted a Samaritan's Purse charity event in New York City. He invited Edward, Dave, Adam, and me to meet Bono and some other celebrities. Dave and Edward chalked it up as a no-brainer and headed down the Palisades to hang out with U2's singer. Bono posed for a picture. Dave stood on his right and Edward on his left. My friends were in their cadet gray uniforms, and Bono was in the middle wearing sunglasses. Adam's tactical officer did not let him go, and I decided that I could not afford to miss class. I was not really sure who Bono was anyway, and that confession has haunted me for years. Apparently, I was the only person on the planet who didn't know about Bono.

I lived a fiercely regimented life as a cadet (and as a human being). I ate at six o'clock every night—every single night. "Scotty eats at six," the others became accustomed to saying. "If you want to eat with him, you eat at six." Adam reveled in being the anti-me. He ate whenever he wanted and didn't eat when others told him to. Adam also knew how to push my buttons. Once, on a car ride back from Georgia, I drove the speed limit and talked about a book I had picked up before getting married. It described the "joys of intimacy." I insisted Dave should read it before he got married. Adam, from the backseat, told me that was ridiculous. "Who needs a book?"

"It's a good book," I retorted. "It provides guidance on how to make your wife happy."

Dave tried to focus on the radio and make the conversation go away. Counter to his directives, Edward was now dating his sister. The whole discussion was more than he could take.

"Scotty," Adam said to me, "you are such a loser. Why don't you live a little and get that speedometer up to sixty-six miles per hour? That way you can get home to read your instruction manual more quickly."

"Fine," I said, "if you don't want to satisfy your wife, then don't read the book."

Chapter 5

WINNING HEARTS

Authentic leaders demonstrate a passion for their purpose,
practice their values consistently,
and lead with their hearts as well as their heads.
Bill George et al., in "Discovering Your Authentic Leadership"

With the dust of Ahmed Said settling and food dripping off the walls in the FOB Marez mess tent, a senior officer grabbed Dave Webb and directed him to confirm deaths and then sort, identify, and bag bodies. As Dave tells it, he wandered out to a vehicle and located a couple of bags. He draped them over his shoulder and forced his feet to take him back to the mess tent. Following orders, Lieutenant Webb wandered through the debris and knelt down beside a body. He rolled the limp corpse from facedown on vinyl flooring to perpendicular, and he stared it in the eyes. Dead. He then dragged the body to the corner opposite Ahmed's point of explosion, shimmied it into a bag as if he were getting ready to take his golf clubs on an airplane, and zipped the bag closed. To his left and right, soldiers were flipping over tables and employing them as stretchers, rushing victims toward medical attention in an effort to save every possible life. It was one of the two worst days of my friend's life, one he tries to forget.

There are several hundred combat infantry companies in the Army, spread out across the globe in places like South Korea, Hawaii, Alaska, Texas, Kansas, Louisiana, Georgia, upstate New York, Germany, and Italy. Each year, West Point cadets toss their white hats into the air, click their heels, and become second lieutenants. After a short vacation, we report to requisite training courses for several months and then transition to our army units. Edward Graham ended up at Fort Bragg, North Carolina. Adam Rivette headed to Fort Carson, Colorado. Dave Webb and I both landed in the same company: Alpha, 1-24 Infantry based out of Fort Lewis, Washington. Chalk it up to serendipity; I saw God's hand at work. I needed Dave during the deployment to Iraq. No one missed his wife any more than I did. In Dave I had a friend with whom I could pray, commiserate, and survive.

Following Captain Jacobsen's death, Dave and I gripped hands more firmly. The mess hall bombing moved combat from an adrenaline-producing movie to full-scale reality. In the months leading up to the loss of our commander, patrols and firefights seemed a bit like a football game: action-packed, exciting, and team-oriented. But bullets and bombs were not free safeties and defensive linemen. I knew that, of course, but now I really knew it.

The genuine danger of it all had never eluded Tiffany. She was a somewhat reluctant army spouse. When I was still at West Point, she suggested I leave and come back to Pasco—become a dentist maybe. But Captain J.'s death notwithstanding, I believed serving our country was my calling. I envisioned a future in the esteemed Ranger Regiment, maybe even Delta Force someday. Military service is a family endeavor to be sure, and the emotional tug-of-war experienced by Tiffany is a common condition for those who support soldiers. She wanted me to be happy, but she also wanted me next to her in bed, safe and warm. I did not want to force on Tiffany a life she did not choose, but I feared the stagnation of a job lacking the kind of purpose I craved. I prayed God would show Tiffany and me where we were to go—what road he wanted us to travel.

Combat turns reflection into a luxury. While Dave Webb bagged bodies, my friend Captain Jeff Van Antwerp—an assistant operations officer—tried to organize the battalion from its headquarters. Jeff is a fearless professional, but he has a huge heart. Moments such as this twist the emotions of even the bravest soldier. Jeff called around to each company, attempting to account for every person in our seven-hundred-person unit. Captain Rob Shaw, who had been with the battalion commander when the mess hall exploded, returned to assist Jeff with the command-and-control efforts.

"Rob," Jeff asked, "I heard there were a bunch of guys from Alpha Company in the mess hall. Did you see Bill down there?"

As Jeff remembers, Rob winced and responded cautiously, "Dude, you didn't hear?"

"Hear what?"

"Bill's dead."

Fifteen minutes later, Jeff stood in front of our battalion commander, Lieutenant Colonel Kurilla. Kurilla explained that Jeff would be stepping in to take over Captain Bill Jacobsen's command of Alpha Company. "You'll be taking the company at 1600 hours," Jeff remembers him saying. This was not the assumption of leadership Jeff had envisioned. He was not supposed to be Bill Jacobsen's replacement.

In an ideal world, or even a sane one, Jeff would have taken command, not of Alpha Company, but of Bravo Company in February. He had planned to spend January refining his command philosophy, and on the day of his ascension he would have delivered rehearsed, but genuine, thoughts to a group of wide-eyed men with the sun slowly setting behind him. Instead, an hour after Ahmed Said altered that scenario, Jeff knelt in his trailer and prayed. He told me he prayed for Riikka Jacobsen and the four children, six and under, who would never see their father again. He prayed for his soldiers, and he prayed for himself. Jeff cried a bit, and then he walked outside and stood in front of us: 120 men who had just lost their leader. He could barely speak.

There is nothing weak about Jeff. He is a warrior who runs two miles in under eleven minutes. He considers anything less than one hundred push-ups on the army physical fitness test substandard. Jeff played intercollegiate soccer at West Point, and with his brother Luke he finished second in the U.S. Army's grueling Best Ranger Competition in 2002. He is charismatic, reminiscent of a Ken doll, but sporting ears that stick out a little more than Mattel would like. Over the phone, Jeff could pass for a high school student, projecting a medium-pitched voice that bubbles with enthusiasm. Captain Van keeps his golden locks a little longer than the average army officer—the hair consistent with the time he spent as an army brat in Hawaii and California, learning to surf.

Upon his introduction to Alpha Company, Jeff Van Antwerp looked us in the eyes and cried, his emotions belying his substantial physical strength and endurance. "I had no choice but to be real," he said afterward. "It was not time to figure out who I was; it was time to be who I was." Jeff loved Bill Jacobsen, and authenticity in that moment allowed all of us to love Captain J. too. Some of us kneeling, some of us bloody, most of us bleary-eyed, Alpha Company had to move on—just like that. "Captain Jacobsen was my friend," quivered Jeff as he stood at the front of our formation. "I will miss him. I am in command of the company now, and tomorrow we begin a seventy-two hour mission."

As Dave Webb likes to describe his cousin—Jeff and Dave happen to be cousins—Jeff Van Antwerp was a devious youngster, whether beating his brother Luke with a whiffle-ball bat or tormenting his sisters with stories of torture chambers in the basement. But at West Point something clicked, and he became a leader, an amazing leader. When Jeff waxes eloquent about the essentials of command, his sentences hum with the words "people," "relationships," and "love." Jeff acknowledges the essentials—physical fitness, tactical and technical competency, integrity, and courage—but underscores that those things render a leader satisfactory. Caring for people makes a satisfactory leader great. "Soldiers run on relationships," argues Jeff, as if love is the fuel that fills our tanks and warms our hearts during ominous nights on patrol.

I believed it. Jeff was a hero in my eyes, a big brother, a companion, and a competent tactician who would never lead me astray. I felt blessed that God had provided for us in the wake of such devastation, sending Captain Van Antwerp to replace Captain Jacobsen.

Jeff mentored me on big-picture perspective. Alpha Company was in Iraq not just to fight terrorism and blow stuff up but to rebuild the community and the economy and earn the trust of the people in Mosul. Captain Van Antwerp spent hours upon hours in the city, ping-ponging between our company's three platoons to sell his vision of change—both to the Iraqi people and to his men.

One day a couple of American tanks rolled into our area of operations. The armored unit was playing hide-and-seek with an enemy sniper and believed they had flushed him up to the minaret of a nearby mosque. Jeff, understanding the consequences of rifling a

120-millimeter tank round into the apex of a mosque, ordered the soldiers to withhold fire. Two minutes later, the deafening boom of a seventy-ton Abrams tank told Jeff those soldiers had ignored him. The tank round not only obliterated the top of the mosque, but the concussion of the blast blew out all of the windows of the buildings to the left and right of the Abrams. I learned from Jeff on that day that a myopic focus on the immediate target could send shock waves through the foundation of larger strategic objectives.

Captain Van worked tirelessly to win the hearts and minds of his soldiers so we would win the hearts and minds of Iraqis. His strength of character—his faith in God—necessitated that every member of our company follow the Golden Rule. The rule applied to Iraqis as well. There would be no revenge for Bill Jacobsen's death, no wanton destruction. Only respect. Jeff's was a difficult message. He was asking us to wander the streets and risk our lives at the hands of an unseen enemy but at the same time to promote kindness and compassion. As Jeff executed his mini-strategy, he also worked to help us stay human—to feel we could still enjoy a bit of life despite the serious nature of everything around us. One day, while my platoon patrolled a main thoroughfare, a foreign noise penetrated the command radio network in the form of a medium-pitched and enthusiastic, if off-key, voice:

You missed a couple of classes and no homework
But your teacher preaches to you like you're some kind of jerk.

And then a pause . . .

You gotta fight for your right to parrrrrty!

In the middle of Iraq, Captain Van was belting out a vintage 1980s rap song from the Beastie Boys. His lyrics weren't spot on, but we appreciated the gesture. Jeff demanded excellence. But relationships and authenticity were still at the heart of his leadership.

Chapter 6

INSIDE NARNIA

"It means," said Aslan, "that though the Witch knew the Deep Magic, there is a magic deeper still which she did not know. Her knowledge goes back only to the dawn of time. But if she could have looked a little further back, into the stillness and the darkness before Time dawned, she would have read there a different incantation. She would have known that when a willing victim who had committed no treachery was killed in a traitor's stead, the Table would crack and Death itself would start working backward."

C. S. Lewis, *The Lion, the Witch, and the Wardrobe*

Every West Point graduate looks forward to serving as a platoon leader, even if the experience lasts only a year or so. Captains, majors, and colonels constantly reminisce about their days as a "PL." It is, according to most, the best job an officer will have. The winter of 2004 and the spring of 2005 was my time in that role—in Iraq, in the middle of a war. Combat had seemed almost fictional when I was applying for the military academy as a senior in high school—before 9/11. But several years later, there I was, in charge of one of Alpha Company's three platoons. Forty soldiers were under my care. Were one of them to lose his life, I would somehow bear responsibility, even if the mission did come first.

I hate to admit it, but exiting the outside wire boundary of FOB Marez with my platoon induced a sort of Pavlovian fear response inside me. As a kid, I read in C. S. Lewis's book about crawling into the wardrobe, through the fur coats, and emerging through the back side into the snowy world of Narnia. Our base at Marez felt safe, even if its safety was imaginary. Narnia—Mosul—emerged mysterious and dangerous, with the unknown around each corner. I judged myself selfish for fleeting thoughts of shirking my duties—running back through the wardrobe and locking it shut behind me. But each day I found the strength to lead and to instill confidence in my team. After I prayed, my Stryker vehicle—an armored green rectangle that sat atop eight giant black wheels—exited in the lead. I always went first. That is one thing I had learned about leadership during my time at West Point and in Ranger School.

Mosul hurt the eyes. This city in the northern portion of Iraq looked a little bit like Pasco. The optimist in me saw it as a slice of home. Except that the people had so little. On the outskirts there were shepherds and farmers who lived in mud, rock, and cement huts. In the urban area, more than 250,000 souls were crammed together into a single square kilometer. It seemed that most of the inhabitants threw their garbage into the narrow streets. When our Stryker rolled through, we veered slightly left and slightly right to navigate the wickets of trash. Human waste sometimes stuck to the tires until worn away by the dirt. The city stunk, daily exhaling a fresh belch of excrement, urine, standing water, and human body odor. I eventually stopped noticing the smell. I just got used to it.

Some of the stories and events from the world that was Mosul were as fantastical as a C. S. Lewis creation, but much more gruesome and difficult to stomach. A preteen Iraqi told me of children who played soccer with a couple of human heads. The decapitated bodies had been dropped off in the street—everything seemed to be dropped in the street. On a different day, our battalion's headquarters, which directed the operations for our seven-hundred-person organization, ordered my platoon to check out a pair of earlier-executed Iraqi fighters. Our team of four Strykers drove across town to search through a graveyard that looked more like a city dump, until we located the bodies in question. We rolled the bodies over, snapped some pictures, and took some notes, and then rolled the bodies back. Both men had been shot in the head several times. It was surreal—scary even—to be handling human beings in this manner. I prayed that I would never get used to it.

My only real retreat from the madness was time with Tiffany—whether on the phone or in my head. I missed the small things, like flirting with her and having her hop into bed. I missed her scratchy morning voice. I talked about her constantly to anyone who would listen, mostly Dave Webb. One night I wrote in my journal: "Dave has been great but nothing can replace Tiffany. I miss her love and desire her so badly." Dave was grateful at that point that he was *not* a replacement. It wasn't all mental snuggling and footsie with Tiff, though. I consider myself the organized one of the two of us and sometimes wondered what was going on with the checking account. I hated worrying about money; I hated talking to Tiffany about money even more. It produced a tension I preferred to avoid. But I obsessed a bit over the bank statement. Tiffany spent most of November and much of December on Oahu with Tanya Webb, Dave's wife. Hawaii was not cheap. According to Edward, Dave, and Adam, I am.

"Dave," I asked. "Um, what's the . . . what's the Silver Moon

Emporium? And why is Tiffany spending three hundred dollars there?"

"Oh Scotty," laughed Dave, "that's a really expensive clothing store on the North Shore. You're suckin'. She probably bought a dress."

"Dave, what is Alan Wong's?"

"Dude, that's a really expensive restaurant. How much?"

"Uh . . . two hundred dollars."

I brought up the shopping and eating with Tiff during our next phone call. "She was very understanding and loving as usual," I wrote in my journal. "I hope that we are able to do something about it and save money. I miss Tiff so much and wish we never had to have these kind of talks over the phone." Then I laid my tired head down and rested up for the next day's mission.

Morning brought another rotation outside the wire. My half of the platoon traveled with Lieutenant Colonel Eric Kurilla, our battalion commander, and the other half went with our operations officer, one of the two majors in the battalion. This was one of the only days that I did not take the lead. Lieutenant Colonel Kurilla—a larger-than-life character who reveled in the challenges of leadership—assumed the point for our group. Our task was to provide security for the commander as he walked the streets and talked to Iraqis. Security proved more difficult than advertised. My commander moved quickly and unexpectedly. I would have had to read his mind to keep up with him. I was once again a linebacker trying to hang with a speedy wide receiver. Kurilla buzzed to the sidewalk and then cut left at the big pile of garbage, stopping at a gas station to question a suspected enemy. Recent intelligence suggested this gas distributor also peddled information to terrorists, and it seemed Lieutenant Colonel Kurilla wanted to know more.

My uh-oh antennas rolled out to an upright position. With the six Stryker vehicles from my platoon pulled over to the curb to the left of the gas station, I climbed atop an adjacent building to scope the surroundings. As I crouched on the roof and peered over its side to ensure no one was preparing an attack, a rocket-propelled grenade (RPG) whirred past my left ear and exploded into a building across the street. Along with a few other soldiers who were on foot, I scurried back to the Strykers. One of the gunners had heard the launch of the RPG and caught a glimpse of the culprit running from the scene. Lieutenant Colonel Kurilla resumed command of the unit and led us in the direction of the attacker. About eight vehicles traveled in a column through Mosul's tight roads, chasing after one or two individuals.

A couple of left turns later, Kurilla's Stryker came to a halt in front of an abandoned car, postured like roadkill in the middle of the street. Our column stacked up behind him, with just a few feet separating each of our vehicles. Silence grew as I stood in the turret of my Stryker, my chest flush with the top of the vehicle, and waited for LTC Kurilla's orders. Then the silence broke. Bullets started to ping off our armored vehicles. LTC Kurilla told everyone to dismount from inside the Strykers (so we would not be killed if hit by another RPG). We pulled to the left of the road and exited the vehicles. The members of our platoon lay down on the ground behind our left wheels—on the side of the Strykers farthest from the road. The Strykers were now our cover—like protective boulders in front of us. Behind us was a row of buildings. To our front was the road and then a deep crevasse. We scanned across the road and over the sixty-foot-wide ravine. We were desperate to figure out where the bullets were coming from.

Head down and feet scampering, I moved from Stryker to Stryker to ensure all of our men were properly positioned. Dust kicked up behind me as bullets trailed my boots. It looked like a scene from a movie—an unrealistic scene where the good guy races across an opening and the enemy lands rounds everywhere but in his chest. It looked like that, except this was completely real. I told my men to fire back—not an easy task when enemy whereabouts remained a mystery. A bullet trail continued to follow me; I figured the assailants possessed AK-47s and maybe BKC machine guns. Their aim was accurate. Fortunately, not Clint Eastwood accurate. The furious *pop, pop, pop* of our weapons filled the air as our platoon sent 5.56-millimeter rounds across the ravine in search of nothing in particular. I ducked behind a Stryker to take a breath. Seconds later, Staff Sergeant Farmer sidled up to me and announced that Villanueva had been shot.

I picked up the cat-and-mouse game again and ran back to Sergeant Villanueva's Stryker, near the back end of the convoy. Two soldiers attended to Villanueva. One knelt on the sergeant's left in a pool of blood; the other soldier crouched on the opposite side, his hands shaking and his face ashen. The sergeant howled in pain. Blood pulsed from his leg and drenched the hands of the pale-faced soldier. When our platoon left the gates that morning, our medic had gone with the other section. No one on site could make Villanueva's bleeding stop. I yelled at the soldier in the puddle of blood to tighten a tourniquet around Villanueva's maimed leg, and if that did not work to put another one on. Fortunately, it took only one. With the tourniquet's tension twisted tight enough to keep Villanueva alive for a short period, I ran back and told LTC Kurilla that Villanueva needed medical attention quickly.

At the front of the convoy, nothing had changed. Soldiers still curved their machine guns around the tires and fired at the ghosts of the ravine. We needed to get out of there quickly. I could not see the enemy, could not provide effective return fire, and I had a man drifting into shock. I felt like one of the plastic targets on a firing range: immobile, defenseless, and doomed. I fired off some rounds in the enemy's general direction and ordered my men back into their vehicles. I told Lieutenant Colonel Kurilla that Villanueva's life depended on an immediate departure for the field hospital. Kurilla okayed the request as backup Strykers arrived to help the commander locate and destroy the enemy. My platoon raced off to save a life, but we did not arrive in time to save Villanueva from permanent damage to his limb.

The world within the wardrobe was far removed from Fort Lewis, and Tiffany, and even Ranger School. I had been scared that day. But I did my job the best I could. I led. I risked my life to direct our platoon. I made the best of a bad situation. Even on days like that one, my soul told me this was my place—with these men, doing this job.

There were good days too. Days when beautiful Iraqi children—with black hair and dark brown eyes—climbed on me like I was back at West Point, teaching Sunday school. Days when I had chances to serve and do what I love: listen, care, and help others. One of my sergeants came to me for comfort because he had lost a friend to the enemy; another came because he could not shake from his head the terror of killing a human being. I listened and I tried to help. Captain Van Antwerp paid me a compliment that I hold close to my heart: "The thing that really mattered was Scotty cared about his soldiers. He loved his soldiers. And they knew it. And they knew it because he gave his time; he invested in them; he shared his feelings with them and they shared their feelings with him." I am not perfect, but I did my best to care for these men.

Selfless service means loving your soldiers. Selfless service also means letting your husband love his soldiers instead of you sometimes. I wrote in my journal 133 times while in Iraq. One hundred and one times, I talked about how much I loved my wife, how much I missed her, and about how much I longed to see her again. I love my wife as much as any man ever has, and maybe because she knew that, Tiffany gave part of me away to the army.

The last time I ever looked upon Tiffany's face was March 17, 2005. I had stopped by Captain Van Antwerp's trailer to ask a question. Jeff just happened to be talking to his wife, Therese, a close friend of Tiffany's, via webcam. When Therese Van Antwerp noticed me in the background, she told Jeff to move aside and let me say hi to Tiffany, who was visiting Therese at Fort Lewis. I had never done this before—the video camera thing on the computer—but it was pretty cool. Part of me was taken by the technology, but most of me was captivated by my beautiful wife.

I thought Tiffany looked more mature and grown-up, or maybe it was just that she'd had her long brown hair cropped to shoulder length. It was so good to see her. I also had ridiculously lengthy hair (by army standards), trimmed just above the ears. It was not that Jeff with his long-haired look expected it that way, but his surfer vibes influenced me silently. A few minutes into the virtual conversation, Tiffany looked over her left shoulder at something. She looked back at me, and then she looked over her shoulder again. Therese, from the background, was scolding Tiff. "Your husband hasn't seen you for months. What are you doing with that coat on? Take it off. Show him some shoulder." Tiffany wore a jeans jacket, but abdicating to Therese's demands, she removed it in favor of a slightly more revealing tank top, showing her gorgeous arms.

The webcam conversation made me long for my wife that much more. Tiffany on a computer screen was great—touching her, lying next to her, and falling asleep with her would be the only thing better. I closed my eyes and prayed for lucid dreams, thankful that I had only a month until my midtour leave.

Chapter 7

GRAY OPEL

Intel says VBIEDs tomorrow. Hope it's not right.
My final journal entry, 5 April 2005

Ahmed Said, the man who blew himself up and killed Captain J., shouldered the blue-collar load in the bombing of the FOB Marez dining facility, but clearly he was not the brains of the operation. Said merely played Pinocchio to someone else's Geppetto. By spring of 2005, Khaled Abdul-Fattah Dawoud Mahmoud al-Mashhadani, known more simply as Abu Shahid, was suspected of pulling the strings in and around Mosul. He deployed up to thirty suicide car bombings in March and April alone. Abu Shahid was part strategist and part producer. He orchestrated the construction of vehicle-based improvised explosive devices (VBIEDs) out of aged gray Opels, human batteries not included. In the meantime, prospective martyrs poured into Iraq like Duracells gliding down a conveyor belt. Abu Shahid paired his VBIEDs with human beings, guided the total packages out to roadside locations, and thanked the detonators for their service to the cause.

Route Tampa—a main thoroughfare named by U.S. Army forces at the outset of Operation Iraqi Freedom—ran south to north from

Kuwait across the landscape of ancient Mesopotamia. A patched-together version of I-95 or I-5, Tampa snaked north to Baghdad and through Baghdad Traffic Circle, shot a northwesterly arrow beyond Yarmuk Traffic Circle in Mosul, about 220 miles from Baghdad, and then continued north before running its course in Turkey. There were no Vince Lombardi or Molly Pitcher service areas along Tampa. It was a naked strip of concrete for the most part, known up north in Iraq as much for its explosions and dangers as for its vehicle traffic.

I read the battalion intelligence report on the morning of April 6. The message was the same as the day before: terrorists had suicide car bombs available and were willing to blow themselves up. VBIEDs were the tactic of choice for al-Qaeda in Iraq. The day prior, our company had lost Sergeant Yoon when a car exploded. He took a blast of shrapnel to the head and had to be evacuated out of the country. There was nothing particularly tempting about a mission that asked us to go searching for car bombs. A combination of trepidation and common sense enticed me to forgo the car-bomb egg hunt and cleave to the safety of the base, but of course that was a fleeting, unrealistic thought. If my men and I did not discover the VBIEDs, then a helpless fuel truck or a critical supply convoy would. Every bomb we found meant a life or more saved.

Our platoon prepared to roll out of Marez at about 11 A.M. My Stryker sat at the front of the convoy as we waited for our exact departure time to arrive. As we waited, my thoughts trailed toward Tiffany. "You know," I said to my squad leader over our internal intercom, "I've been married now for sixteen months and I've only seen my wife for four of them." I could hardly wait to get home for my midtour leave.

When departure time hit, we exited the base and headed for the

Yarmuk Traffic Circle, where five roads converge spokelike into a central wheel. Captain Van Antwerp traveled along with us. I established a small protective element—single soldiers perched atop buildings—to monitor the frenzy of Yarmuk, and then, along with Jeff and the rest of the convoy, I returned south to strike up some conversations with locals and seek out the VBIEDs. Jeff told me to keep my platoon off Tampa and to avoid traveling on the smaller, east-west roads as well: Porsche, Nissan, Honda. "Travel through the less built-up areas," advised Captain Van. Traveling south, using Route Tampa as a handrail, we crossed over Route Porsche and then about a half mile later crossed over Route Nissan. A few hundred yards after we crossed Nissan, Jeff received an updated intelligence estimate. Iraqi civilians whispered that terrorists were preparing a massive ambush somewhere in our area of operations. The enemy purportedly forced a row of shopkeepers out of their buildings on the east side of Tampa (in the vicinity of where we had just traveled), setting up a linear launching point for a westward attack. Upon receiving the news, Jeff broke off with his vehicle, U-turned north back toward Nissan, secured a safe location, and dismounted to walk, talk, and gather information.

I continued northward with the rest of the platoon (we were three Strykers in all navigating small side streets to the east of Tampa), retracing my route back toward Yarmuk Traffic Circle through a forest of old buildings that resembled a suburban strip mall, only bleaker. At some point, the side streets became cumbersome. The intelligence—that several car bombs were in the area—was fresh and time was at a premium. We exited the side streets and moved back onto Tampa, heading north at a quick pace. About fifty yards shy of Porsche, I slowed our element a bit and pulled the two other vehicles into a wedge—a Stryker slightly behind on each of my flanks. Three U.S.

Army combat vehicles, like a flock of migrating fowl, crawled north toward Porsche as I surveyed the scene. My plan mirrored Jeff's. I would dismount, walk south through the shops of interest, shaking hands and asking questions. Then I would meet up with Captain Van Antwerp somewhere in the middle. But before I could pull us to the side of the road to dismount, I noticed something unusual. Just to our right, on the west side of the Tampa and Porsche intersection, a gray Opel sat with its backside dragging on the ground.

I knew this area well. We were now just a few hundred meters south of the Yarmuk Circle, surrounded by a fruit market made up of nondescript tan and gray buildings. At midday, traffic normally buzzed in the vicinity of Tampa and Porsche. On April 6, it was just the solitary gray Opel and a few civilians wandering along the side of the road. My Stryker turned right onto Porsche and approached the Opel. The front of the car was facing us as we traveled west to east and pulled up so that we could see into the front seats. As best I can remember, Porsche had no median. It was a four-lane road, divided only by a painted line. The vehicle was about twenty yards to my left. A thirty-something Arab man sat in the right-side driver's seat with a ten and two grip on the steering wheel. He seemed out of place. His car seemed out of place. He had pulled to the far right side of the road and nestled against a curb. My Stryker crawled some more, until I was in a position to look him in the eye. I yelled for him to get out of the car as he glanced in my direction. He just stared at me.

Chest high in the turret with Oakley M Frames perched on the brim of my nose, I won the stare-down. The man raised his hands off the steering wheel, spread his fingers, and faced his palms forward. His lower and upper lips compressed and his cheeks puffed out as if to say: "I'm a good man—nothing to see here." I wondered if the man was lost. This was not exactly tourist country, but travelers did sometimes pass through to find family or visit the shops. *Maybe this guy is waiting for someone to give him directions?* Slow revolutions of the gray Opel's tires interrupted my thought process. The man and his car were now crawling slowly, headed west on Porsche, from right to left in front of me. I yelled again, but his crawl continued. Maybe he was going to keep driving west for a few more yards and then take off across Tampa and into the distance? I wasn't sure what he was running from, but his behavior made me suspicious.

Rules of engagement dictated that I fire my own rifle only if the man first employed lethal force or communicated a legitimate intent to use lethal force. This scene seemed odd, but not yet lethal. I pointed my machine gun toward the road in front of the car's hood and squeezed the trigger. Nearly simultaneous with a tiny pop from my rifle, a small cloud of dust rose just to the left of the car's front bumper. The Opel stopped and the man again elevated his hands. Then the driver spread his arms wide and turned his head to the left, looking in my direction as if to say something. But I was not sure what he was trying to say.

"I don't have a bomb"?

"I don't have a gun"?

"You don't need to shoot at me"?

Maybe all three?

Five seconds passed, and the Opel inched forward again. I noticed the man had a shaved head, trimmed probably with a razor blade and then allowed to grow for a week. The length of his facial hair matched the length of the hair covering his scalp. He had dark skin with Chia-pet black across his chin, cheeks, and upper lip. I thought about ending this game, but the rules of engagement still said no. I processed the circumstantial evidence: car bomber. But maybe there were two kids in the backseat? Did I really want to shoot this man and live with the consequences if I was wrong about his intentions? A $300,000 West Point education told me to do the right thing. The man leaned his head and the upper part of his torso toward the steering wheel in a bowing motion. He still had not threatened. The car continued inching to the left, rolling away from me and toward Tampa. But with our other two Strykers covering the intersection, we had him surrounded.

I fired one more warning round into the road. This time, the man did not raise his hands.

PART II

The Interim

Chapter 8

FOREVER BLACK

I have been driven many times upon my knees by the overwhelming conviction that I had nowhere else to go.
Abraham Lincoln

Just a few minutes into his meet-and-greets with shopkeepers, Jeff Van Antwerp heard the world explode, a blast so loud he told me it sounded as if it could have come from the building next door. The Opel and its driver disintegrated into a million pieces. A small chunk of shrapnel took a direct path to my head, obliterating my Oakleys and dissecting my left eyeball like a blade slicing through a grape. The metal debris continued straight forward, completely through the retina, and penetrated the front portion of my brain. Inside my skull, another tiny piece of metal, the size of a deer tick, took a sharp turn, skipped across the back side of my nasal cavity, and shredded the optical nerves and fibers on the right half of my face. My body recoiled, lurched forward, and then dangled from the turret. A puff of smoke rose from the corner of Tampa and Porsche as my world went forever black.

Jeff has shared with me many times what happened next. He abandoned his conversations and sprinted back to his Stryker, where Sergeant Loepfe gave him the news: "Two-one has been hit."

("Two-one" was the call sign for my Stryker vehicle.) In an act of expediency, Captain Van Antwerp ignored his own Route Tampa warnings and navigated the most direct route to our location, pushing his vehicle to its sixty-mile-per-hour limit. He arrived to see a smoking crater where the Opel once sat. Car pieces littered the ground. One of my squad leaders had been knocked unconscious and our machine gunner had taken some shrapnel to the head—but my injuries appeared to be the most serious. As my apparently lifeless body hung from the turret, my equipment vest snagged on a piece of metal, blood pooled below my feet on the floor of the Stryker.

Fellow crew members, noticing the bloody mess on the right side of my face, screamed for assistance. They unhooked my vest from the turret, moved me away from the Stryker, and bandaged my head—mummifying me for protection. My pulse was faint. I was hanging on to life as my platoon mates loaded me up for transportation to an aid station.

Jeff jumped into the medical evacuation vehicle with me. The ambulance sped to a combat support hospital, where doctors rushed me to a CAT scan machine to examine my head. As my body disappeared behind a pair of swinging doors, Captain Van says, he fell to his knees. Casting aside inhibition in the middle of the hallway, with doctors and nurses scurrying around him, he cried out in agony. He prayed with abandon, yelling out to God, begging Him to spare my life. "People were asking me if I was okay," Jeff said later. "At that point, was I supposed to be the *strong* commander? *Whatever.* I was broken."

A surgeon emerged from behind the two doors, walked forward, and planted himself in front of Jeff. Captain Van rose to his feet, rubbed his eyes, and focused on the doctor. A squad of my soldiers stood behind Jeff, wondering if I was going to make it. I had been slipping toward death, and doctors were using drugs to keep my heart rate up. As Jeff remembers it, the doctor, bereft of emotion perhaps due to daily exposure to death and destruction, said, "Well, doesn't look good. Most likely he'll lose both his eyes, and he's got shrapnel lodged in his frontal lobe." Then the doctor turned and walked away.

Jeff spun, slammed through a swinging door, and slumped into a heap outside the hospital's front door. With his back against the exterior of the building and his head between his knees, Jeff says, he thought about Tiffany. He would be calling her soon, calling her before someone else she didn't know could deliver news she did not want to hear.

Jeff clinched his fists and closed his eyes. We were the closest of friends. We loved each other. Captain Van Antwerp acknowledges the cultural prohibition on such fraternal commander-and-platoon-leader closeness. But we had connected instantly when we lived as neighbors in Dupont, Washington. He never thought he would be my commander, but even after Ahmed Said changed all that, Jeff's friendship with me didn't impact our professional relationship. It was a non-issue with the other officers in the company, because Jeff loved *all* his soldiers. Everyone was his favorite.

But now, as he sat in the dust while I was reeling inside, sightless and clinging to life, it was Jeff's love for me as his friend that poured out. We had worked out together every single day in Iraq, pushed each other to extreme physical limits—one more rep, one more crunch, one more mile. When we could spare a moment, Jeff, Dave Webb, and I would square off in testosterone-filled combative bouts, reminiscent of sixth-graders using one another as Play-Doh in their parents' basement.

I know Jeff trusted me as a leader as well as a friend. He believed in my character. If my men spent two days at an outpost with no latrine, no hot chow, and constant boredom, I would be there with them. When the inaugural Iraqi elections came around in early 2005, Captain Van Antwerp had assigned my platoon an extremely difficult mission. He charged us with establishing and securing a voting site on the outskirts of Mosul in one of the province's most violent locations. It was a built-up area, accessible only by foot. If an enemy attacked, he would be difficult to pursue. But with minimal guidance we secured the area and thousands of Iraqis voted democratically and lived to bear the fruits of their political participation.

Sure, I was kind of a black-and-white thinker. My strength of conviction manifested itself, at times, as an inability (or unwillingness) to understand nuance. My whole life had been framed in terms of good and evil. Jeff had to beat that out of me a bit. He did, because I wanted to learn from him. The more I fell in love with the army, the more I wanted to learn and do. Jeff was a great teacher.

Captain Van joked, months after the injury, that the only noncommissioned officer who ever had a problem with me was this one guy who complained all the time. He was not really a bad guy—the sergeant—but I didn't tolerate complaining. I just didn't do glass-half-empty—even if the glass only had a drop left.

As Jeff waited at the hospital, thinking over what he later told me were some of our most important memories, a soldier from my platoon tapped him on the shoulder. I had been unconscious for a few hours now, temporarily staying at the field hospital in Mosul before the doctor finished up his assessment and processed me for transport. Once I was ready, Jeff and our company first sergeant loaded me and the ventilation tube that snaked down my mouth onto a Black Hawk helicopter that would shuttle me to Balad, Iraq, for surgery. Jeff patted my arm, turned, ducked, and cleared the radius of the Black Hawk's rotor. The helicopter lifted into the air, and just like that my combat tour was complete.

Jeff returned to the battalion headquarters, grabbed the satellite phone, and walked out behind the battalion headquarters shack to call Tiffany.

Chapter 9

INNER STRENGTH

When peace, like a river, attendeth my way,
When sorrows like sea billows roll;
Whatever my lot, Thou has taught me to say,
It is well, it is well, with my soul.
Horatio G. Spafford, "It Is Well with My Soul"

Hope Amelia Solo was not always a goalie. Although she would eventually mind the net as the starter for the U.S. national team (and earn a shutout to secure the gold medal in the 2008 Olympics), Hope started her soccer career as a forward. She amassed 109 goals at Richland High School in the late 1990s, led the Bombers to a state championship in her senior year, and was twice named a *Parade* All-American. Then Hope Solo went to the University of Washington and became a goalkeeper—maybe because she grew tired of defenders like my wife.

Doug and Karen Elliott raised a son and three daughters. The first-floor study where Tiffany sat and waited for an e-mail after the Mosul mess hall bombing is now a shrine to my in-laws' athletic accomplishments. White-and-purple Pasco Bulldog varsity letters—forty of them maybe—wallpaper the room. Between the four of them, Travis, Tiffany, Nicole, and Michelle played five different sports. Until senior year, when she shredded her ACL on the first day of basketball practice, Tiffany had planned to play college hoops, college soccer, or both. Michelle, the youngest in the family (at least, a few minutes younger than her twin sister), did grow up to play college basketball, at Gonzaga, winning two West Coast Conference titles and twice being named the Zags' Most Inspirational Player.

My father-in-law has long believed that had he been able to bioengineer a combination of Tiffany and Michelle, he could have manufactured a superstar, capable of dunking home the winning bucket in an NCAA or WNBA championship game. In his test tube, he would have mixed two parts Michelle's athletic ability and three parts Tiffany's fire and determination. On the court and on the field, Michelle was talented but nice. Tiffany was not quite as talented and not quite as nice.

Just ask Hope Solo. Or ask Tiffany's third-grade teammates. Even at nine years of age, Tiffany was a ball hog. The coach would tell her to pass; she would glare back and hold on tight. When she wasn't dribbling or shooting, she would run down the court, screeching, "Give me the ball! Give me the ball!" People were shocked to see cute little Tiffany, a petite blondette with an angelic look, sliding across the floor, leaving thin slices of her knee on the free throw line. When Mom Elliott noticed Tiffany's halo turning from mellow gold to blood red, she says, she would slouch a little in the bleachers and look around shiftily to see if anyone noticed the family resemblance.

In high school, Tiffany's antics had turned from hogging the ball to making every move tough on her opponents. She would often talk trash in soccer and basketball games with competitors such as Hope. But Tiffany wasn't all verbal intimidation. Battling a rival high school during her sophomore soccer season, Tiff shoved the other team's star player to the ground. From the sidelines, Travis Elliott barked with approval, entertained by the spectacle of his sister's toughness. The opposing coach was not as amused, interrupting the match and rushing onto the field to scream at Tiffany. The coach also happened to be the player's mother. The referee quickly separated Mom Coach from a defiant Tiffany and doled out yellow cards to both.

A couple of seasons later, in the final game of her high school soccer career, Tiffany matched up against Hope Solo for what would be their last competitive encounter. Tiffany fought hard, wearing out Hope's shins and fracturing her own arm, but Richland and Solo emerged victorious, stealing a win in overtime and moving on to an eventual state championship.

Mr. Elliott was well familiar with Tiffany's tongue, and the shoving, and her aggression. As an irrepressible three-year-old, Tiffany had stood separated from a collection of sheep by an annoying electrical fence. She sized up the wire barrier and figured in her little brain that crawling under the bottom strand would be the best way to get to the animals. Despite her dad's instructions to stay out, and despite three shocks from that fence, he says, Tiffany managed to crawl through and get to those sheep. That sort of determination is another thing that I absolutely love about my wife.

In the early morning of April 6, 2005, Tiffany slept alone at her parents' house. Her room—the same room she'd had in high school—was on the second floor, just to the left of the top of the stairs. The stairs run down to the entry door of a traditional-looking farmhouse, with a small deck that spans the length of the home's front side. The Elliott residence sits alone on several acres in rural north Pasco. It has a stadium-sized swath of land out front, separating a two-lane country road from the house itself. Splitting off from the road is a long driveway that borders the right side of the yard and ends at a basketball hoop just to the side of the garage. Mr. Elliott, the only other person home on the morning of April 6, slept downstairs from Tiffany, in the master bedroom.

The phone rang at three forty-five. Middle-of-the-night calls were no longer a surprise really, just a gentle announcement that I was checking in. What did throw Tiffany off guard was the sound of a voice that was not mine. Originally hunching her right arm upward and snuggling the earpiece between her shoulder and her head, Tiffany perked up to an L-shape when she recognized the sound of Jeff's voice. She awoke quickly, but had no time to cycle through the possibilities in her head. "Hi, Jeff, what is it?" she asked cautiously.

"Scotty's been hurt pretty bad."

Jeff described in as much detail as possible what had happened to me, where I had been injured, and where I was headed (to a hospital in Germany after some surgery in Iraq). "There's metal in his eyes, and they don't know if he is going to make it." Jeff's voice trembled. Tiffany sensed he was holding back tears. My wife had always seen my commander as a portrait of strength. His apparent pain was her clearest indication that something was life-changingly wrong. "I'll call you when I get more information," Jeff continued, and then his voice broke. "I'm sorry, Tiff. I'm so sorry," Jeff poured out. His tears echo in her mind to this day.

Not yet able to cry herself, Tiffany stood up and walked to the stairs. She sat down on the top step, teetering between devastation and shock. Through a window she rarely looked out, one above the entryway door, the headlights of a lone car cut right to left across Tiffany's front. No one needed to turn down the driveway, she told me later.

Tiffany already knew something really bad had happened. But hours would go by before she knew any more.

Tiff rose from the top step and woke up her dad. She called her mom. She called Therese Van Antwerp. She called her sisters. She called my mom and dad. One by one she told them, "Scotty's been hurt." Once she had called everyone, once quiet reemerged, Tiffany did break down and sob. Tiffany's dad could not see the future, but he had seen his daughter skin those knees and go after those sheep. It was nowhere near time to utter the empty assurance that she would "be okay," but Tiffany's dad knew his daughter would endure. She had an inner strength and a foundation of faith that would help her surmount whatever was to come.

In Mosul, Jeff began what he has described as a marathonlike struggle to come to grips with my injury. For the next two weeks he did not laugh, he did not smile, and he did not cry. He showed no emotion.

"Would it have been easier for me if you had been killed?" Jeff has asked. "I don't know. I don't even know," he explained rhetorically. "There's something about the finality of death; there's sort of a closure there. With Bill Jacobsen—he was gone. We mourned him. But because I didn't know what was going on and what the outcome was going to be, I couldn't stop thinking about you and Tiffany and what your future held."

He continued, "I don't know why it was so much different with you. There were guys who were shot dead standing two feet away from me. And I loved that guy. Loved that guy. And he was dead. But with you, I knew you were never going to see your wife again. I just didn't know how to deal with it. All the guys in the battalion kept asking how you were doing. It was the hardest thing I've ever been through."

Surgeons at the American military hospital in Balad moved rapidly to save my life and mitigate the long-term impact of my traumatic brain injury. The shrapnel stuck in my left frontal lobe had placed my life in peril, but the swiftness of my evacuation from the battlefield lowered the danger level from grave to worrisome. A multihour operation that removed the metal from my brain and repaired my damaged dura mater (a thin but tough layer just underneath the bone of the skull) also left my brain badly swollen.

To guard against the potentially fatal implications of untreated swelling, the doctors next executed a craniotomy. They sheared my hair (something I think back on with sadness—I was proud of my hair), gently sliced through a layer of skin (tracing from the midpoint of my outer ear to the peak of my head), peeled back my scalp, cut through some muscle, and then removed the front left quarter of my skull. To preserve the hand-sized portion of bone flap for future use, the doctors next cut open the left side of my abdomen, just above the hip, and slid the piece of bone into a newly formed kangaroo pocket. It was supposed to stay there in my side for half a year, waiting to be removed, and when the swelling in my brain receded, that slice of my head could be placed like a puzzle piece back in its rightful location.

While doctors tended to my brain, eyes, and skull, Tiffany's family trickled into her house one by one. Her mom returned from a trip to Portland. Her sister Nicole came back from a friend's house. Her brother drove across town. The clock ticked slowly and loudly. There was not much to say. Apparently, someone suggested that Tiffany get a passport, in case she needed to rush to Germany to be at my side for the last time. Or—unspoken as it went—in the event that she needed to escort my body home.

At around breakfast time, Tiffany received her second update, an unorthodox but welcomed call to her cell phone from a doctor in Balad. He shared the results in the wake of the craniotomy: after clearing the metallic debris from the inside of my head, the surgery team then completely removed what remained of my left eye and sewed my right eye shut. It was not clear to Tiffany why exactly the medical practitioners had troubled to suture my right eyelid closed, especially if I had "no real hope" to see again—but even confusing news was better than the uncertainty that had filled the previous several hours.

From an "Is he going to live?" standpoint the rest of the doctor's report moved Tiffany's attention from curiosity to anxiety. I was not retaining fluids, and the surgeons could not restore my blood pressure to normal levels. I had not yet escaped death. The doctor from Balad also suggested Tiffany secure a passport in anticipation of a trip to Germany. And when that doctor hung up the phone, Tiffany says, it was maybe the most real moment of her life. She felt in ways she had never felt; she employed emotional muscles she did not know she had. *Seriously? Is this happening? How am I going to live?* I absolutely forgive Tiffany for slipping into selfishness for an instant. The bond of marriage turns two into one. My blindness suddenly became her blindness. The next fifty-five years of my life became the next fifty-five years of hers.

The gray Opel and its driver were not what shattered Tiffany's world—she had been sleeping peacefully when they burst into a meteor shower of shrapnel and knocked me unconscious. The subsequent cell phone call with a doctor's assurance that I would never see again was *her* moment of pain. Just after sunrise on a Wednesday morning in Pasco, gravity of circumstance pulled Tiffany's entire future into a tiny blip of the present and collapsed the life she thought she would have. The explosion engulfed a nursing career, dreams of a family, a second honeymoon—it even robbed her of the compliments I would pay her smile. "For better or for worse" once meant that I sometimes came home grumpy. Those five words would soon take Tiffany somewhere altogether unimagined.

CHAPTER 10

ONE SQUEEZE

The Lord is near to the brokenhearted
And saves those who are crushed in spirit.
King David (Psalm 34, verse 18)

My younger sister Mary Lynn looks a lot like my mom. She has the same jet black hair and bright blue eyes, so bright they almost appear to be glowing. She is my closest sibling in terms of age, by a year and a half, and back at Pasco High School we used to spend a lot of time together. She usually hung out with my friends, which was cooler than me hanging out with her friends. It was never really a big deal to me that Mary Lynn took German in high school. Mary Lynn said "everyone took Spanish," and she did not want to be everyone. She tried to enroll in French, but a hiccup in her schedule forced her into German instead, and because of that high school scheduling fluke, my little sister ended up by my side as I held on to life at Landstuhl Regional Medical Center, a U.S. Army hospital near Ramstein Air Base in Germany.

Landstuhl is tucked in the southwest corner of Germany between the Rhine River and the intersection of Luxembourg and France. It was also a two-hour train ride north of where Mary Lynn was living for a few months that spring of the explosion. As she had grown increasingly fond of German during high school and then college, Mary Lynn decided she wanted to visit the country and learn even more of the language. Six months after her graduation from the University of Washington in January 2005, Mary Lynn landed in Frankfurt, traveled down to Freiburg, and enrolled in the Goethe-Institut, a German language school.

I departed Iraq eight hours, one craniotomy, and an extracted left eyeball after I had arrived at the hospital in Balad. My mode of transportation switched from helicopter to airplane, but the speed of the flight meant little to me—I was still unconscious. I don't remember a thing from those moments after the injury.

Back in Pasco, word spread quickly among my family members: "Scotty's been hurt." My mom and dad woke up my sister Kathleen and my brother Nick. My parents called Stephen, Krista, and Neal. Neal called Edward Graham. Edward called Adam Rivette. And finally, Mom e-mailed Mary Lynn. We have recounted the events and figure that Mary Lynn clicked open the e-mail message Thursday morning at an Internet café in Freiburg. With a crowd of mostly Turks around her, she processed the words on the screen: "Scotty has metal in his eyes. We are not sure he is going to live." Surely those gathered in the café stared in confusion as Mary Lynn slipped into gyrating panic. She ran from the computer screen to a phone and called home. Somehow she remembered that injured U.S. soldiers made a midpoint stop in Germany on the way back to the United States.

"Dad," Mary Lynn asked, "is Scotty coming here?" When she found out I was en route to Landstuhl, my loving little sister launched a burst of logistical creativity. She had a high school friend, Peter Francik, who was serving in the air force at Ramstein. She thought, *I need to get in touch with Peter,* she told me later. I cherish Mary Lynn's sense of caring and determination. She tells a story of desperately needing to get on a train. All she could think about, she says, was that she needed to be with her big brother. Hers was the kind of love and support that would lift me up in my lowest moments. I am so thankful to Mom and Dad for building such a tight-knit family.

Mary Lynn explains that she raced to a friend's house, a woman she had been nannying for part-time. She spoke in broken, blubbery German: "My brother's been hurt in the war. A bomb exploded. Metal went in his eyes. I need to call my friend in Ramstein." Frauke, the German friend, helped Mary Lynn get online. They found a phone number for the air force base and dialed an operator. "My brother's been hurt. I need to talk to Peter Francik." Ramstein is home to thirty-four thousand military personnel—the request was quite preposterous. But somehow the operator found a number and Peter answered. He told Mary Lynn he would be there when she arrived at the station. He would take care of whatever she needed.

Within an hour, Mary Lynn was on a train. She says that she just sat there: praying, crying. A German man next to her apparently grew uncomfortable with her outward expressions of grief. But Mary Lynn needed to talk to someone. She looked at him intermittently, providing sufficient discomfort until he asked what was wrong. "My brother has been hurt in the war. But he loves God, and I know it's going to be okay." From what I have heard, the topic of religion is a close runner-up to Iraq in terms of joyful German conversation pieces.

"I'm sorry," he replied. "That's terrible."

The moment the doctor from Balad told Tiffany there was no real hope I would see again, she admits to me, her denial quickly transitioned to confusion. *How are we ever going to do anything? I don't know any blind people. I didn't marry a blind guy.* The thoughts possessed her for hours—until the next update.

As the train sped Mary Lynn toward my side, another doctor, from Germany this time, called Tiffany in Pasco. "If we can't start getting him to hold fluids, and if we can't get his blood pressure up, he might not make it. You should prepare to come to Landstuhl." The message was clear: I might die. Tiffany recalls that she heard the word "passport" more times in those twelve hours than in her first twenty-four years combined. She climbed back up the stairs, veered left through her door, and collapsed on her bed. The phone call from Germany—the one making it crystal clear that I stood at death's door knocking—popped the balloon that held her remaining strength.

After what Tiffany tells me was twenty minutes of crying, she rolled off her bed, knelt, and prayed. Only God remembers her specific prayer. Tiffany recalls that she asked for peace and understanding. She asked that God be with my doctors. And then once again, she asked for peace and understanding. Sometimes God delivers His promises over the course of forty years, and sometimes He answers in four seconds. As if she'd touched Jesus' cloak in a crowd, a warm spirit of calm rushed through Tiffany's body. She felt the peace she had just requested. "If you died," she explained to me later through tears of love, "I knew that I would be okay. And if you lived, I knew that God was going to use your life for great things. And at that moment, in some way that I can't explain, I felt like I had no preference. Somehow I trusted God that much. I trusted that either way, you would be okay. And I would be okay too."

Tiffany's unwavering strength, faith, and love from that point forward testify to the reality of God's presence in our lives. She understands if you don't understand. She really does. It all sounds a little bit mystical, but Tiffany knows, for sure, that God grabbed hold of her that day. He answered her prayers in a tangible way—sent forth a physical presence that replaced fear and doubt with trust and strength. To the believer, it's believable. To the questioner, it's questionable. And that's okay with Tiffany. It really is. Man . . . I love her.

Mary Lynn, the most emotional of my three sisters, burst into tears, more forcefully this time, upon sight of Peter at the railway terminal. Peter was someone who actually knew me and understood how much my sister hurt. He raced Mary Lynn to the hospital, where the staff brought her to see me. Bandages draped my head, face, and eyes. To her I looked like the invisible man. A breathing tube pierced the layer of bandages and protruded from my mouth. Machines pumped fluid into my puffy blowfish of a body. The only humanity Mary Lynn could see, the only way she even knew it was me, was my profile. That was a Smiley nose, a clear identifier.

Mary Lynn signed forms, authorized a blood transfusion, called Mom and Dad, and advocated for me. She says that she prayed. She cried. She prayed. And then she cried. None of the other patients had families present, so she prayed for everyone she could find. Sergeant Yoon, the Alpha Company soldier who had been injured the day before me, was also at Landstuhl. Mary Lynn prayed for him too.

On Friday afternoon, doctors removed my breathing tube. Mary Lynn recounts that my body coughed violently in response to the change. She needed physical contact with me to calm her own nerves, to feel like she was being of some use, so she began to rub my marshmallow feet. I don't remember her touch, but I know I must have felt it, and her love must have comforted me. Who knows? Her presence may have even saved my life. Though I couldn't process what was going on at the time, in the years since, as we have recounted the ordeal, my love for my sister (and for all my family and friends) has deepened in ways I cannot express. In the greatest crisis we have ever faced, my sister raced to be by my side. How blessed a man I was to have my little sister there holding my feet.

A few hours after removing the tube, the doctors forced me "awake." I was not lucid, even if no longer medically asleep, so I still don't recall if I understood that it was my sister giving me a foot massage. As Mary Lynn's hands worked the muscles at the base of my toes, a nurse told her I might never be the same. I had experienced significant brain trauma—trauma that might have altered my personality. Mary Lynn prayed once again, that the brother whom she loved would still be the same man who crumpled forward in that Stryker vehicle.

Tiffany asked Mary Lynn to find a way for her to communicate with me. "When he comes out of it," Tiff said, "call me. I want to talk to him. I want to know if he knows me. I want him to hear my voice." Once awakened, I guess, I had the wherewithal to communicate nonverbally. I was able to squeeze once for "yes" and two times for "no."

"Can you hear me?" Mary Lynn asked. One squeeze from me. "Can you feel this when I poke your right leg?" Two squeezes.

When the routine questions subsided, Mary Lynn called Tiffany and held the phone up to my right ear. From thousands of miles away, Tiffany cut through the muting effect of bandages and shined a light through the fog in my brain: "Scotty, do you know who I am?" Slowly, I squeezed: once for yes.

"I love you Scotty." Tiffany cried in desperation.

Then, fighting her trademark tears, my sister whispered to me,

"You love her too? You love her too, Scotty?" I squeezed my swollen appendages around Mary Lynn's palm . . . once for yes.

Yes. I love her.

I wish now I could remember that moment, but I can't. I am grateful Tiffany has that memory with her to this day.

CHAPTER 11

SOME SOLDIER

The extreme and terrible nature of war touches something essential about being human, and soldiers do not always like what they learn. For those who survive, the victors and the defeated, the battle lives on in their memories and nightmares and in the dull ache of old wounds.
Mark Bowden, *Black Hawk Down*

Mary Lynn never had a specific moment of transformation, but over the course of three days, my little sister evolved into my protector. Her entire identity shifted from vagabond tourist to my personal concierge. Every ounce of her energy had gone into my emotional care. She says it was like a mission—she would not leave my side. When Mary Lynn received military orders to fly back to the states with me, necessity forced a brief separation. Peter Francik drove Mary Lynn to Freiburg, where she collected a couple of weeks' worth of clothes, and then she returned to Landstuhl for flight preparations.

My sister remembers that she bundled up in layers of sweats for a trip, the comforts of which would be a bit below economy class. To the only civilian on that floating infirmary, the guts of the C-17 looked like a prison camp. Bunks were stacked ominously in the middle of the plane. The beds rose three units high and were loaded with invalid heroes whose conversations frustrated Mary Lynn.

"I got shrapnel in my leg."

"The blast took my finger off."

Mary Lynn says she considered lashing out. *My brother is lying here half dead. He is never going to see again! Be quiet with your comparably insignificant problems.* She understands the insensitivity of her thoughts, but Mary Lynn was wound so tight, thirty-four thousand feet above the Atlantic Ocean, that a release of her stress could have turned that C-17 into the *Hindenburg.* Once again, Mary Lynn stood next to me and rubbed my feet. Once again, I had no idea. I do not recall a thing, and even if I did, I might not have felt her rubbing. In addition to the loss of my left eye and the craniotomy, the right side of my body had been paralyzed by the blast.

"The Lord and adrenaline kept me going on that plane," says Mary Lynn. She gritted her teeth and tried to lose herself in some music as she stood by my side. She also prayed for Tiffany—whose coming encounter with me was sure to be an emotional challenge.

The screeching of rubber impacting concrete and a subtle jolt informed Mary Lynn that we were *home*—in a sense. The large gray plane slithered along the ground at Andrews Air Force Base until coming to a stop next to a bus. Attendants rolled me out the tail end of the plane and loaded me onto a coach that had been gutted of its seats. Mary Lynn remained trapped in the bowels of the plane. "Wait," she yelled, "that's my brother. I am supposed to be with him!" But I was already settled in on a bus reserved for intensive care patients.

"Ms. Smiley?" interrupted the voice of a civilian woman. "This way, please." Mary Lynn boarded a different bus. She tells me her next thought startled her. *What am I doing here? I am supposed to be in Germany.* The entire seventy-two-hour experience had robbed my sister of every ounce of her spiritual strength. Now, somewhere inside she was acknowledging her part was over. Mission complete. She had brought her brother back to the United States. Safe and sound.

Walter Reed Army Medical Center has the distinctive look, the requisite lack of architectural imagination, of a federal building. It's a gigantic, multilevel, square structure—tons of cement trimmed with dark glass, nestled in a small Washington, D.C., neighborhood between Georgia Avenue and Sixteenth Street. The soldiers inside the gates are missing limbs, licking wounds, and hearing voices. At Walter Reed, much of the first floor is occupied by the "Warrior Clinic," dedicated to the care of "Warriors in Transition."

The entrance to Walter Reed is impressive—regal even. Everyone who would eventually visit me walked into the building and passed under enormous red-and-blue flags that stick out from the left and right walls and hang twenty-five feet above the ground. Apparently, the entrance area looks something like the United Nations Headquarters, except the flags represent esteemed military units: the 82nd Airborne, the 10th Mountain Division, the 1st Armored Division, and tens of others. Behind the flags, vertical wood paneling rises forty feet from the floor to a bunkerlike cement ceiling. The walls and the ceiling do not really match. The walls give off a 1980s corporate boardroom vibe; the ceiling suggests Walter Reed is part care facility and part nuclear protective bunker.

Past the last of the flags and coming out from the wall straight ahead is a third-floor overhang. The balcony looks fit for the pope on Easter or for the president on Inauguration Day, but really it's where family members stand as their loved ones enter Walter Reed en route to their rooms. My dad remembers watching me come through the front doors that day. Tiffany says they weren't allowed to stand up there. We're not certain who is right. The trauma of such circumstances makes it tough to recall exact details. No one had seen Mary Lynn for several months. She had been in Germany traveling and nannying. And our family can't remember exactly if or when they saw her that day.

During my three days in Germany, the doctors had stabilized my condition. The craniotomy had allowed my brain to swell and recede without severe damage. Tiffany didn't need to fly to Germany, and by the time I arrived at Walter Reed, my eyesight was more of a concern than whether or not I would live. But my wife tells me she still didn't know exactly what to expect.

A scared Tiffany touched the door of the surgical intensive care unit (SICU), unsure what I would look like on the other side. A number of friends would travel to see me in the coming weeks. My coma, my traumatic brain injury, and my blindness would hang over the lives of those closest to me for months and years to come. My injury apparently touched people all over the world, in and out of the military, and I thank all of them for their love and support. But only one other person on the planet would feel the full repercussions of that terrorist's actions for the rest of her time on earth. From the moment she opened that door, my wife would begin a ride with me that would endure forever. Once their pain had subsided, others—even my parents, my siblings, and Jeff Van Antwerp—would be going back to the lives they had lived prior to the injury. My mom and dad would always hurt for me, but they wouldn't be driving me to work every day or taking care of our children. In the end, this was one amazing woman's battle. Tiffany was alone with God, me, and her fortitude. I understand perfectly her reticence to reach out her arm and push that door open. She stood there for a moment, wondering if her life with me would ever be what it once had been.

Looking back on our honeymoon, an all-inclusive resort getaway might not have been the best choice for a pair of newlyweds who rarely drink alcohol. But financial considerations aside, Tiffany and I enjoyed the hassle-free convenience of Jamaica's Grand Lido Braco Resort: no bills, no tips, no arguments. Our first vacation together sputtered to a difficult start when the dreadlocked man behind the counter announced there were no regular rooms available and suggested we accept accommodations on the "free" side—also known as the naked side. I liked free and was pretty sure I was going to like naked, but only if it was my wife, me, and a bedroom thing. Dead tired from our travels, Tiffany and I accepted the "free"-side room for one night under the condition that we would receive an upgraded suite on the side for modest people for the rest of our stay.

We fixed our eyes on the flowered shirt of a Grand Lido bellman and followed the sound of our rolling luggage through a bar until the tinging of a steel-drum band drowned out all other noise. As Tiffany's eyes glanced left and right away from her plodding feet, she saw flab, breasts, and thighs. The sights turned Tiff's face into a giant tomato. When I caught a glimpse of her embarrassment, pulsing commenced in a vein just above my right temple. "Sir," I called out with my head down. "Sir, we are going to need to turn around." The man slowed the luggage cart to a stop, grimaced at me, and waited. "My wife and I, um, we want to go back and wait for a normal room."

As the bow of the luggage cart turned around, naked guests began to mock us. “They're just kiddos,” a middle-aged woman chuckled as she tapped the bare shoulder of the guy next to her. “True enough,” he responded, “they haven't seen anything like this before.” Nope. Tiffany and I had never seen anything like this before, and it took us just a few seconds to decide that we never wanted to see anything like it again. We returned to the front desk and settled for a room smaller than the one we had paid for, happy that our vacation neighbors were all wearing clothes.

In front of the Grand Lido, white sand beaches melt into aqua blue waters that sweep out to an unreachable horizon. Behind the colonial-looking buildings that make up the main part of the resort, green vegetation litters the Jamaican countryside. The Caribbean in December was a far cry better than Pasco, Washington. Tiffany and I spent the first few days snorkeling, waterskiing, lifting weights, lounging, and holding hands. We spent the public part of our nights sampling international cuisine and talking our way into deeper friendship.

I dedicated a couple of hours each day to repeatedly falling off a windsurfing board and gagging in Dixie cups doses of the salty ocean. My inability to spend even a few seconds skimming across the water with back arched and sail filled earned me a dubious reputation among the daily beachgoers. I was the guy who couldn't windsurf. Outwardly, I cast my crooked smile in the direction of my new friends. Inside, my lack of coordination drilled a huge hole in my gut. The irony of me—with the benefit of full sight—hopping aboard a surfing instrument in calm Jamaican waters and repeatedly disappearing into the blue lagoon would come full circle a few years later.

I awoke on Christmas morning 2003 just before sunrise. Jamaica was beautiful for sure, the most gorgeous place I had ever experienced.

But its trappings were simply a sideshow to the woman beside me. What I treasured most about my honeymoon was the pinch-myself feeling of spending the entire night with Tiffany in my arms. I could really lay down my head, fall asleep, and rest knowing that she would be there when I awoke. It was everything I ever wanted. As I looked over her body that morning, she had just the right amount of muscle, perfect touches of soft accentuation, and the cutest freckles a man could ever hope to touch. But I didn't have to hope. I could touch the freckles, kiss her lips, and welcome my wife awake to Christmas in Jamaica.

With darkness still covering the beach, Tiffany and I snuck outside our back door and tiptoed through the soft sand. Chirping birds welcomed the morning as we laughed our way to the right spot. Fifteen feet up from a calm tide, we lowered ourselves to the ground and sat together, Tiffany between my legs with her head against my chest. I wrapped my arms around my girl, still amazed that we were here, husband and wife, in this place. The sun crept slowly up from the far reaches of the ocean and peeked out from behind a cloud. As the natural light of the Jamaican morning broke the darkness, I opened up a Bible. With Tiffany listening, knees tucked to her chest, I read aloud about Jesus' birth. We ended the morning trip to the beach with a request that God bless our marriage and protect our love.

Tiffany's hand forced the SICU door to swing back to the left and she took a step into the tiny room, large enough for just twelve of the most critically wounded patients in an army approaching half a million. My bed was the first one on the left, tucked between the SICU's exterior wall and a yellow curtain to the right. There was more machinery than person in my cubbyhole: tubes, wires, monitors, and metal. What stood out to Tiffany was the way the permanently inserted catheters (PIC lines) disappeared into each of my shoulders. A third PIC line shot into the femoral artery in my left leg. I had a tube up my nose. I was pathetic enough that a few days later my mom would be feeding me as she had when I was eleven months old, sliding the spoon under my lip on its way out of my mouth to clean up any leftover rice cereal. It was, for my mom, a surreal experience, but she came to grips with it pretty quickly. She told me later that if we had had to live that way for the rest of my life, it would have been okay, because we are here on earth for just a while. My mom's faith is truly incredible.

When Tiffany knelt in her bedroom in Pasco and was instantly filled with a peace from God, she knew that somehow all would be okay. But as she turned the corner and took in the sight of her decimated, dependent, lifeless husband, she admits to me, she had no idea how it would be okay. Still, Tiffany shook off her despair and walked toward my nose, the only thing that she, like Mary Lynn before her, could recognize. Seven steps later she was standing at my side. "Hi, Scotty."

I reached up with my left hand, maximizing my physical abilities, and petted her hair. "Hi, Tiff." Words were coming now but only in pairs—I was in a medically "awake" state but still do not have any recollection of that time. Apparently I was in no mood for conversation—a first from Tiffany's experiences with me. Fortunately, at that moment "Hi, Tiff" was everything she needed.

"Hi, Scotty. I love you."

As I said, I do not remember the exchange. Tiffany will never forget it. Tiffany had her ambitions—you don't hog the ball in third grade, accomplish what Tiffany did as an athlete and a student, and grow up to just waft through life. My wife is a strong, courageous woman who didn't marry me to be my caretaker. She could have been focused on all that she was losing. But in the Walter Reed SICU, surrounded by beeps and blood pressure monitors and eleven other wounded veterans, Tiffany's desires were not about her own ambitions or even my ambitions—she simply wanted me to know who she was. That's all she hoped for. And I did. Even if I didn't know it at the time.

Tiffany collected the rest of my family from the fourth-floor waiting room and brought them in to see me. My mom remembers most clearly the pain felt by Stephen, my older brother just above me in our family. "I looked back, and there was Stephen slumped down on the floor in tears. That was the hardest thing for me," my mom recalls. "Seeing one of my boys lying there hanging on to his life and my other strong son crushed by the sight of it all."

My mom's faith inspired a similar strength in each of her children. Her daily admonitions to read the Bible produced a discipline of spirit that feeds the Smiley soul. What I took from my dad was a drive toward perfection. You should see his new house (even though I haven't really seen it). Everything is in exactly the right place, done exactly the right way. I've felt around the kitchen, and the garage, and the master bath, and I know my dad well enough to imagine how everything looks.

My dad stood over me at Walter Reed to give me a kiss and tell me that he loved me. What I whispered in his ear, as he recalls, was: "Some soldier, huh?" Lying there, world changed forever, I was not proud of my service, bitter about my fate, or self-loathing in my misery. I was embarrassed. "Some soldier, huh?" If eloquence had been at the ready for me, I likely would have visited a refrain that would soon become familiar: "Look at what I *can't* do now." I didn't have the mental wherewithal at that moment to question my faith—to despair about what my life would look like as I wandered around helpless in the dark—but the three words of shame I expressed to my father said enough for the moment. *Some soldier, huh?*

Chapter 12

MEDICAL RETIREMENT

Would you prefer to be blind or deaf?
Book of Questions, #171

I spent the next week at Walter Reed essentially unconscious. In my mind, I was still in Iraq. Tiffany says that I would ask about my men. I would see things in my head and try to shoot at them. When my weapon failed to fire, I would reach out in an effort to defeat the enemy hand-to-hand. I ordered the doctor to find my sunglasses. "Where are my Oakleys?" I screamed. "I need my Oakleys!" After unrelenting requests, a doctor finally brought me some glasses. I'm told that I wore them for two days straight.

While I don't remember anything I experienced externally during those first few days in Walter Reed, I do recall some of my dreams. I was going to an airport. And then I was going over water. I would yell at my men to watch out, but in my dreams I could not move. Someone in my dream told me that I was going to Washington, D.C., and I got excited. I dreamed of being in the backyard of the White House—getting out of a limousine and shutting the black doors behind me.

Three days into my hospital stay, doctors had me moved from the SICU to Ward 58. I occupied room 5831, located straight back from the entrance to the ward with what they told me was a nice view of some trees (not that it mattered to me). An army of emotional supporters shuffled in and out to keep me company, pushing the capacity of the room. My brothers Stephen and Neal were especially diligent, spending nights with me so Tiffany could get needed rest. Jeff Van Antwerp's brother Luke also spent many nights by my side.

One of the fights sapping Tiffany's strength involved my future in the army. Making the safe assumption that a blind man would be moving on to civilian life, a pair of army administrative sergeants began shuffling papers in front of Tiffany with directives to "sign here." The sergeants explained the basics without going into unnecessary detail.

"Once you have signed the final papers tomorrow, we will begin the process of medically retiring Lieutenant Smiley from the army," she remembers them telling her. "He will then become part of the V.A. system, and we will move him from Walter Reed to another hospital." The sergeants' job was to expedite any obvious dismissal case out of the army medical system and into the V.A. system. Tiffany, as a young lieutenant's wife, was an easy case. Blind guys, of course, don't serve in the army. Get my wife to sign, and move me on.

But uneasiness began to gnaw at Tiffany. She grew indignant, believing the pressure to sign those papers was being instigated by people, not necessarily by God. God may have other plans in store for me. Her gut told her not to sign.

Tiffany turned to Colonel Kevin McDonnell, a trusted friend and mentor to Neal, me, and many others. The colonel met many from our circle of friends when we passed through Fort Campbell as cadets, successfully navigating scuba training under his tutelage. Colonel McDonnell strikes a serious pose, as one would expect from a career Special Operations officer. He is articulate, professional, and his words ring with the theme of higher calling—everything is always about something else: duty, honor, country.

"Kevin," Tiffany cried, "they are trying to get me to sign these papers—to retire Scotty from the army. And I'm not sure that's what we are supposed to do. I don't want to make that decision without him. I don't want to sign these right now."

Colonel McDonnell, working in the Pentagon at the time of my injury, recognized quickly what Tiffany needed: advocacy. He implored her *not* to sign the final pieces of paperwork, and he leapt into the fray to provide Tiffany assistance. Kevin's defense mechanisms of choice were a pair of army enlisted soldiers whose office was just a few doors down from the SICU at Walter Reed. The "Thompson Twins," as they have been nicknamed, ensured that every wounded special operator received proper treatment, both medical and administrative. I was not a member of the Special Operations community, but Kevin could not have cared less about that. Tiffany said that he asked the Thompson Twins to put me on their list and to ensure that I received the treatment I needed. In the process, they secured Tiffany some room to breathe and think.

Seven days into my stay, I woke up for real. That is, I began to process some of the things that were going on around me. The first thing I remember is my dad giving me a kiss good-bye—he was heading back to Pasco to tend to the family business. Once able to speak coherently with the doctors and with Tiffany, I communicated two key points:

(1) I can't feel anything on the right side of my body, and (2) I can't see. Until this awakening, I had been protected from the trauma of my blindness—I could respond to people, but I just wasn't aware. Then I came to. Imagine waking up in a hospital bed, thousands of miles from where you believed you were supposed to be (leading your soldiers in combat), and in an instant realizing the world is permanently dark. I'm sure there are other injuries that may be as life-altering as blindness, but I could not think of any. The devastation I felt is beyond words. I cried. I cried tears from eyes that no longer served any other purpose.

When I was done crying, my grief folded into anger. *God is the one who allowed this to happen.* I believed in this God who told me I could do all things. I believed He loved me. But the anger was overwhelming. *Is this how You treat someone you love? You leave them lying in a hospital bed a pathetic wreck?* My newfound consciousness hurled me toward depression. There began a fight for my heart that would last weeks, months, and in some ways, even to this day. I'd read the Bible and believed it. But lying there in the hospital, I wasn't sure what I believed. I wasn't sure I could understand a loving God. I felt betrayed.

The sappy symphony of praying friends, praise songs, and hollow laughter that occupied my room made me want to puke. Those around me, the friends and family who came to provide emotional support, can be easily forgiven for their Bible-reading optimism. None of them had any more experience with never seeing again than I did. Balloons filled the room, Christian music spilled from the radio, and travelers moved in and out as if my room were Reagan National. The doctors and nurses had no idea what to make of it all. As the circus swirled around me, I erupted inside. I couldn't see faces, share nonverbals, or even walk off my anxiety. The sounds of happiness circling the room attacked my sanity. *All of these people acting so happy—well, none of you are living my life. You aren't blind! If God loves me, explain to me why He did this.*

I felt guilty then, and feel guilty now as I remember questioning God in such a way. It goes against everything I grew up believing. But what you believe can change when your world is blown apart. I couldn't run from these feelings or thoughts. I didn't even want to pray anymore.

Edward Graham, who was there in the room, along with Paula Van Antwerp (Jeff's mom), Adam Rivette, my brother Stephen, and several others on that first night of consciousness, asked me if I wanted to pray before Tiffany and the others left to return to the hotel.

I shook my head. No. I did not want to pray. Edward's faith flashed before him. He shared with me later that fear ran through him. He says he kept thinking: *Scotty has to pray.* Tears began to drip from his eyes. *Scotty has to pray. He has to.*

Chapter 13

RANGER SCHOOL

Never shall I fail my comrades. I will always keep myself mentally alert, physically strong and morally straight and I will shoulder more than my share of the task whatever it may be, one-hundred percent and then some.
From the Ranger Creed

Edward Graham and I forged our relationship with weekly climbs from the back side of West Point's mess hall to the Cadet Chapel. The enormous rectangular structure, which looks more like a *Lord of the Rings* fortress than a place of worship—towers above the campus at the crest of a mountain of stairs. The chapel's front-side landing is home to West Point's best view, providing a vantage of the barracks, parade grounds, academic buildings, library, baseball field, and the Hudson River. On an agreeable day in midfall, the scenery from the chapel landing paints one of the prettiest pictures in the world.

Inside, the Cadet Chapel was like my second home. It felt reverent, disciplined, and serene—the way I wanted to live. I tried to express my approach to life with Edward and our friends. In our group of four, my role had always been clear. The three others tell me that I kept them on track spiritually; I glowed in the dark and emitted a loud "Turn here now" (in an attractive British voice) when someone strayed off course. It was a role I had confidence in as a cadet. I grew up in the middle of seven kids. I often had to fight for extra dessert or even just for a spot in the backseat. I wasn't shy about sharing my thoughts with my peers. And given the spiritual foundations my parents had provided, sharing my faith was one way I expressed myself.

Edward, Dave, and Adam called me "the Oak," because they said they always knew where I stood. I pulled off the role, I guess, with a combination of sincere character and naïveté. I loved doing things like teaching Sunday school—spending those mornings swinging my arms and hooting like a creation from a Maurice Sendak book while having second-graders draped all over me.

Never had my role as the Oak been put more to the test than in Ranger School, an adventure I tackled in early 2004, just two weeks after my wedding. Ranger School, headquartered out of Fort Benning, Georgia, is an optional course for most in the army, but a requirement for infantry officers—something I needed to complete before arriving at my unit and leading soldiers.

The army designed everything about Ranger School to hurt. It consists of sixty-one days of sleep and food deprivation, physical exhaustion, and mental kung fu. More leadership course than small-unit tactics training, Ranger School crams a wad of humility down your throat. The ego check began with an inviolable packing list. Two bars of soap: check. One small mirror: check. One set of fingernail clippers: check. Ten pens: check. Two rolls of black electrical tape: check. Two pairs of boots and ten pairs of wool-blend socks: check. Optional items included cotton underwear, moleskin, a lighter, and noncaffeinated chewing gum. Attempting to slip in any form of tobacco, Gore-Tex socks, Tylenol, or contact lenses was grounds for immediate dismissal.

My bags were assembled, inspected, and situated in the corner of my small Fort Benning apartment at seven o'clock the night before Ranger School. When Edward walked in through the front door, I could tell that he was dealing with some doubts. The specter of my cylindrical duffel bags, stacked and ready to go, made Edward feel inadequate, he says. He was not yet packed.

Following a run to the post exchange to round out Lieutenant Graham's packing list, Edward and I settled in for a good night's rest. It would be our last solid night of sleep for more than two months. Preparation, trust in the Lord, and an optimistic spirit served as my Nyquil. Within minutes of flipping off the light switch and pulling the covers to the base of my neck, I was out. Edward, on the other hand, apparently suffered from a case of Ranger-onset insomnia. Map terrain features, Swiss seats, and mud-filled obstacle courses danced in his head; he stared at the darkness. Once his eyes adjusted to the lack of light, Edward read the texture of the ceiling for the better part of an hour. He tells me that all I did was snore, while he tossed, muscled his eyelids down over his pupils, hoped everything was in his bags, and looked again at the clock. When the alarm finally jolted me awake, Edward said he had slept maybe a total of two hours. It would still be the most sleep either one of us would get for a long time.

On the first day of Ranger School, Edward and I stuck together. A Ranger instructor (RI) barked out for one-third of the students to move left, one-third to stand still, and for Edward, me, and about forty others to move right. Once divided into a platoon, our group broke down into smaller squads. Still together at the end of the first day, Edward and I would stay that way for the duration of the course.

Edward's insomniac doubts tagged along with him through the first week. His insecurity came partly from a debilitating knee pain.

Advancing the ball down the pitch during an intramural rugby game at West Point, Edward got clipped from the side by an opponent, tearing the anterior and posterior cruciate ligaments in his right knee. He spent the next six months, including most of his time up until Ranger School, regaining ligament stability through the restriction of a gawky, mechanical knee brace.

Georgia in January is not Alaska, but it is still cold. Edward told me his knee was killing him. Plowing his way through the bayonet assault course on a day when the thermometer topped out in the low forties, he ground to a near halt. The knee locked. No wonder he was in agony; both of his ligaments had been ripped from the bone in that rugby game. I could tell that Edward was in incredible pain. He was a tough guy, but this injury, combined with the cold, was getting the best of him. Tylenol was not on the packing list.

"Ranger," an RI barked at Edward, "what exactly is your problem? You better get your weak butt moving through this assault course or you'll be done here and gone real quick." His inability to even flex his knee in the cold weather convinced Edward that Ranger School would be a short ride. He sat down to the side of the bayonet course, with his freshly shaved head in his hands, and told me that he didn't think he could make it.

"Can I pray for your knee?" I asked. "Lord," I whispered as I laid my hand on Edward's leg, "please take care of Edward. Take away the pain that is in his knee so that he can make it through Ranger School. Amen." Later that night, back at our bunks, I pulled Edward aside, touched him once again, and prayed. Edward woke up the next morning and his knee worked. It never hurt again. I thanked God for His faithfulness.

As the field portion of Ranger School began, I decided to do all that I could to help the others, whether that meant packing bags, sewing on name tags, or praying. I wasn't trying to draw attention to myself. I just felt like these were the things God would want of me. During the swamp phase, the platoon had to construct a one-rope bridge across a chilly body of water. The RIs asked for a volunteer. It was thirty-four degrees outside, and this was just a refresher class—it was not even a real pretend mission. Before the RIs could "volun-tell" somebody, I detached my right arm from my leg and raised my hand into the air. *What am I doing?* Sure, I had been through scuba training as a cadet, and I had been a lifeguard. I was a pretty strong swimmer, but it was thirty-four degrees. In the end, I spent twenty minutes bathing in that swamp and fastening a rope to each side of the shore to serve as a bridge. For whatever reason, I felt like my strength was holding and that God wanted me to help.

The first phase of Ranger School faded into the second, but not before the platoon received a two-hour break. In preparation for our time off, Edward and I sent Edward's mom a letter asking her to come down from North Carolina and visit with us. "Bring food, drinks, a phone, and a smile, Ms. Jane," I requested. "You have never let me down, Ms. Jane. Don't let me down this time." The letter, however, made its way to the mailroom looking like a neglected orphan. The glue on the envelope got wet, so Edward secured the edges with black electrical tape. I scribbled on the address. It would do, except that when Ms. Jane received the messy prodigal envelope, apparently she feared its contents. Anthrax scares had circled the country a few years back, and Mrs. Graham says she did not recognize the handwriting on front. She tossed the letter onto her passenger's seat and left it.

I could bear some extra weight on road marches, endure some cold temperatures, and use some sleep time for prayer, but the one thing I could not stand was being away from Tiffany. When I had the chance to talk to my wife, I could barely breathe. While my head was on a swivel, frantically looking for Mrs. Graham in a Fort Benning parking lot during our two-hour break, Edward spotted Dave Webb. Living at Benning and still attending the Infantry Officer Basic Course, Dave thought that Edward and I might need some company and showed up with a car and a phone. We inhaled some Whoppers, fries, and milk shakes, and I got my chance to call Tiffany. Crisis averted. (Mrs. Graham opened the letter a couple days later.)

Those who successfully navigate Ranger School become expert "droners." They can walk half asleep, rest while upright, and catnap for the briefest of moments while propped on one knee. I never mastered droning, and one evening that failure became evident. Edward was just in front of me on a standard, late-night Ranger patrol. Stepping quietly through the woods, he says, he heard me muttering behind him: he claims he could hear me talking to Tiffany. "You were apologizing to her and being all lovey-dovey," Edward insists. "You were like, 'I'm sorry, Tiff. I'm sorry.' Kissing her and stuff. When I yelled at you to be quiet, you just told me to shut up—that Tiffany was going to get mad."

I don't think it ever happened. Edward swears that it did.

The final phase of Ranger School took Edward and me to the heights of the Tennessee Valley Divide, somewhere in the peaks of northernmost Georgia along the Appalachian Trail. February at an elevation of three thousand feet brought fifty-mile-per-hour winds and a blanket of snow four inches thick. The platoon slogged up a hill, dressed only in our camouflage uniforms and combat boots. Some of us wore gloves; others breathed a sigh of relief when their fingers became too numb to feel. The chill of the air and the power of the wind created icicles that hung parallel to the ground.

At the crest of a mountain, our patrol knelt to rest. Edward mentioned the sweat that had gathered on his undershirt during the ascent of the slope. The sweat was chilling his chest, his toes were freezing, and his hands were thawing. They ached as the blood coursed through contracted veins on the way back to his heart. Edward could not have been more miserable. There had been a few moments like these during the first month of Ranger School, and each of them brought the same prayer. "Please, Lord, put me out of my misery," was Edward's request.

Neck bowed and hands pulled to his face, Edward blew warmth onto his fingers as the wind slapped his face. The horizontal icicles crashed to the ground. In the distance, far below me, lay the expanse of the Tennessee Valley, draped in a combination of white and green. I prayed: "Thank you, Lord. This is beautiful. It is gorgeous." Then I turned to Edward. "If we were not at Ranger School—if we were just out here in the snow—think about how beautiful all of this would be. It's God's creation." Edward knew I was right, but it would take him at least four more weeks to admit it.

Edward pressed on. I encouraged him, and myself, that we could do all things through Christ.

About 50 percent of those who begin Ranger School end up graduating; that ranks it as one of the most selective military courses in the world. Prospective Rangers are eliminated for failing leadership missions, proving inadequate on basic tactical tasks, and coming up short on the initial physical assessments; and sometimes their peers vote them out. Those who don't fail outright may start over because of an injury: frostbite, dehydration, insect bites, or more serious things.

Only 20 percent of those who report to Ranger School graduate in the minimum sixty-one days. In March of 2004, Edward Graham and I made that 20 percent cut together. The God who strengthens provided Edward and me the fortitude we needed to earn our tabs.

At each graduation ceremony, a freshly minted Ranger recites the Ranger Creed in front of friends, family, the cadre, and the chain of command. The creed is an indelible part of Ranger culture—more than a collection of six stanzas to those who wear the tab, and a way of life to those who actually serve in "the Regiment." A stammer or a misspoken word by the Ranger reciting the creed in front of the crowd would be a point of significant embarrassment, prompting the colonel to command a right face and order a set of push-ups—at graduation, in front of everyone in attendance. On rehearsal day, I volunteered to make an attempt and be the speaker. It was a stupid move on my part. I sometimes have trouble remembering my phone number or the names of all my siblings. During Beast Barracks at West Point, I never even managed to memorize all of my plebe knowledge.

On graduation day, Edward looked on quizzically as I scaled the platform steps en route to the microphone. I bent over, looked out at my fellow graduates, pronounced the first three words, and stalled. Then I stared into space and muttered something nonsensical. Within seconds, I was facedown on the platform, doing push-ups.

CHAPTER 14

FOR WORSE

And straightway the father of the child cried out, and said with tears, "Lord, I believe; help thou mine unbelief."
The gospel according to Mark (chapter 9, verse 24)

Edward and I had been through a lot together, but lying in the bed at Walter Reed with the world gone black, I didn't care how much Edward wanted me to pray or whether anyone was counting on me. When I could see, I had done things I was proud of, like getting through Ranger School and having a good experience doing it. But that part of my life was over. Now I was just a disabled guy whose head had been sliced open. I was in my own fight with God—if God was out there somewhere. I bottled up my torment and lay in silence. I didn't even have to close my eyes to avoid connection with others. For whatever reason, my doubts, anger, and lack of faith were more than I wanted to expose. There was still a small part of me that didn't want to let anyone down, but I also didn't want to give in to their joy when I didn't have any. So I didn't pray, which probably said everything anyway.

Tiffany volunteered to pray instead, but as she prayed, I interrupted her. "I don't know how to pray right now," I said. "I just don't know what a relationship with God means. Let's not do this." I couldn't see

Tiffany's reaction, but I imagine my words stung her like nothing I'd ever said before. Right then, I honestly didn't care.

Tiffany has explained to me that in that moment, her heart contracted to a tiny pea. She could live with a blind man, she was pretty sure. At least, she was talking herself through what it might mean. Walking to and from Walter Reed, Tiffany had been praying to God out loud. People passing by would stare at her quizzically, but that was her turn not to care. Her prayer conversations soothed her pain. During a particularly stressful trip to the hospital, she just kept repeating the phrase "For better or for worse." All of this, Tiffany figured, was "for worse," and she was going to be there in it. There was no question. She told me she resolved right away that come what may she was going to stick with me through it all. It is what she promised me she would do, and even stronger than the spoken words of her promise was the commitment of her heart. She loved me that much.

In Tiffany's mind, "for worse" equaled blind. She hoped I would still be me even if I couldn't see. But when I communicated that I didn't want to pray—was not sure I believed and maybe no longer shared her faith—she realized that that me would not be the man she loved. I would not be her rock. She tells me often that the tremor that ran through her when I told her I didn't know about God and that I didn't want to pray rivaled the call from the doctor in Germany in terms of emotional shock. Tiffany collected her bearings after what sounded to her like my proclamation of disbelief, kissed me good-bye, and headed out the door.

Once Tiff left, I piled on. "What? Tiffany's leaving?" I asked Edward, who had stayed behind to be with me for the evening. "I guess she doesn't want to spend any more time with her pathetic, blind husband." My words came from a place of fear. Not only did I fear that God had abandoned me, or had never been there in the first place; I feared that I would soon be just some sympathy piece to my wife. These feelings of despair and insecurity fought for ownership of my heart. After years of optimism, they were my new reality.

Before I could finish my criticism of Tiff, Edward leveled me, setting aside any pity my injury might have earned me. "Shut your mouth," said Edward. "Your wife loves you. She's been here every night. Every day, Scotty. She's been praying for you, worried about you, and taking care of you. I don't want to hear you say something like that ever again." Edward had something at stake in this too. His own faith had an umbilical connection to mine. He says that as he walked into the grand entrance of Walter Reed, past the flags and the wood paneling, he pleaded with God: "Let Scotty still be Scotty." He was not sure how he'd react if his friend—the Oak—drifted toward disbelief.

But I wasn't some "Oak." The clean mouth and the Bible reading and the churchgoing, those things weren't faith. I mean, they weren't a show. They were an expression of my faith, and I had really believed. But now I didn't know. I couldn't hold on to that belief for Edward or anyone else. It was God himself I was wrestling with. My faith was supposed to be in *Him*. I had a relationship with Him. I felt that faith slipping away from me, and I was caught somewhere between guilt for doubting and resentment for having ever believed.

When Edward completed his rant, my anger suddenly folded back to grief. I brought my left hand to my worthless eyes and bawled, unsure how the pain and sufferings of my current condition were ever going to result in a normal life. I had been here once before, although those earlier circumstances now seemed trivial. But I had been here before, at the precipice of a real crisis of identity. During my first week at West Point, a five-foot-five cadet had stood in front of me and ordered me to straighten my posture. "New Cadet Smiley," she yelled, "get your head back and your shoulders out. You are the worst new cadet at West Point. You don't have a single bread crumb of your knowledge memorized. What is your excuse?"

I wanted to tell her I was smart but that I just didn't memorize well. That the whole *major* outranking *lieutenant* but *lieutenant general* outranking *major general* was justifiably confusing, and that it didn't matter if I knew the difference between a rear admiral and a vice admiral, because I wouldn't see one for a long time, and if I did, I'd just salute and say, "Beat Navy." But I remained silent. I just pulled my shoulders farther to the rear of my pecs and felt for the cement wall with the small of my back. As I straightened up my six-foot-two frame, I looked at the college junior standing in front of me, wearing a gnarly scowl, and responded, "No excuse, ma'am."

"That's right, there's no excuse, Smiley. There's no excuse for you. Now go to your room, look at your knowledge again, and get back out here and do it right. This is your last chance."

I was not sure what came after my last chance. Room restriction? Walking the area? Death? But the consequences of my forgetfulness were less important than making it to my room before I lost my composure. "Yes, ma'am," I replied as I scurried across the hall and turned the doorknob. I opened the door, slid inside a muggy, barren barracks room—with just two desks, two beds, a mirror, and a linoleum floor—sat down on my gray blanket, wiped the sweat from my bald head, and held back the tears. Just a few weeks before, I'd been everybody and everything at Pasco High School. I'd finished an athletic career that would years later land me in the Bulldog Hall of Fame. By June of 1999, people on the streets were still throwing me high fives for the state championship victory over Marcus Trufant and Tacoma's Wilson High. I *was* Pasco High School (or so I thought). I'd certainly never stood in the halls and been yelled at before.

Wondering who I had suddenly become as a plebe at West Point had been disorienting. It had been a trial run (albeit a much less significant one) for lying here in my hospital bed and asking myself who I was as a blind man. At West Point, I'd come to realize that things had changed, but God still loved me and I could still accomplish things—even pass chemistry. At Walter Reed, I no longer believed it. I didn't believe God still loved me, and I was certain I could do almost nothing at all.

From what Tiffany has told me, she made up for the prayers I failed to pray. For the two weeks following my injury, she had been living moment to moment. She considered the future, but she didn't stay there for long. Once, sitting next to the fireplace with family and friends at a long table in Macaroni Grill, Tiffany had watched a blind person walk through the front door of the restaurant. She noticed a guide dog that a month ago she would have ignored. *That can't be my husband. He can't look like that.* Thoughts of her life to come were both energy-draining and depressing. Now that I had reacted so coldly to her as she prayed and told her I didn't know about my relationship with God, she realized she was at ground zero. Kneeling next to her bed in her hotel room after leaving me with Edward, Tiffany met God head-on.

"Lord," she begged, "nothing else matters. I don't care about Scotty's eyes. Just give him a heart for you. Help him to hear you, feel you, and trust you. Please God, renew what was in him before."

Though my world was black now, there was a very small speck of vision in my right eye. I had not thought much about the speck. The ophthalmologist had not even bothered pointing the pen into my left eye socket. There was nothing in there. But when he bent over my bed and shone an arrow of light into my right eye, I saw something! It was a tiny something—like a train at the end of a long, dark tunnel—but it was something. The doctor didn't quite understand how I had seen the light. Based on the condition of my optic nerves, my eye should have been completely unresponsive. The shining of the light had been standard procedure. But even a glimmer of hope, literally and metaphorically, required action. The ophthalmologist recommended an emergency attempt to repair my right eye. He tempered our expectations—chances were there was still nothing that any human being could do to bring me back to the sighted world. But the doctor said he would try.

"If we are in there for a long time," Dr. Dick told Tiffany, my mom, and me, as we recall, "that's a good sign. It means I'm making progress. If I come right back out within an hour, well then, there just wasn't anything that I could do."

The pin of light and the hope that came with it made me regret my lack of trust. Maybe God was just looking for faith the size of a mustard seed? While I gained some hope, Tiffany guarded her emotions. She told me the last thing she wanted was to anticipate the return of partial vision only to endure a cruel letdown. Besides, she would gladly trade my sight in return for a spark in my heart.

I learned later that four hours into the surgery, my mom and Tiffany started to become optimistic. The doctor had said it himself: *If we are in there for a long time, that's a good sign.* Two hundred and forty–some minutes was a long time. The two women who loved me as much as anyone on the planet gripped hands and prayed that I would emerge from that room with one working eye. Even shapes and shadows would be better than nothing at all.

When four hours became eight hours, there was almost a level of surety inside Tiff and Mom. *The doctor had said it. The doctor had said it.* Had Dr. Dick emerged from the operating room in ninety minutes, Tiffany would have bowed her head, exhaled, and moved toward acceptance. But it had not been ninety minutes, or even three hundred. I was in major eye surgery for almost an entire workday. Surely, the pinhole of light would soon be vision anew.

Chapter 15

ANDREW HARRIS

Little ones to Him belong;
They are weak, but He is strong.
Anna B. Warner, "Jesus Loves Me"

More than eight hours after he had begun, the doctor stepped through two swinging doors and walked toward Tiffany and my mom. Tiffany says her mind went blank as she waited for more life-changing news. "I am sorry." The doctor grimaced. "I did everything I possibly could. I still can't explain how he can see that speck of light, but it will never be any more than that. I am so sorry."

Tiffany felt the lump grow in her throat as heat rushed to her cheeks. Her faith did not leap off a cliff in the same way that mine had, but she was certainly confused. Why the temptation to believe in the miraculous? Had not the simple pain of all that had happened been torture enough? Eight hours of waiting had been enough time for a flower of hope to fully bloom. *God loves me? God loves me not?* Tiffany scuttled her doubts. She would not allow herself to join me in the questioning.

It would be the next morning before I shook off the anesthesia and received the news myself. My mom hid in the visitors' lounge as Tiffany hunted down the doctor. Neither of them wanted to deliver the news to me. Once Tiffany had escorted the doctor to my side, she stood back and braced herself. The doctor leaned over the bed and whispered into my ear.

I heard tears in the doctor's voice and tuned out the actual words. It was the single worst moment of my life. I had dared to believe that my existence could be a little less useless. One eye would have been a party compared to no eyes at all. But the doctor nailed that coffin shut. There would be no seeing. I was officially, 100 percent, a blind man.

On the day of the doctor's news, the actor who played Lieutenant Dan from *Forrest Gump,* Gary Sinise, along with Toby Keith and the Secretary of the Army, stopped by to say "hi" to soldiers and thank them for their sacrifices. I told Tiffany to tell them to go away. I didn't want anyone in my room—no actors, no musicians, no civilian leaders. "But it's the Secretary of the Army," said one of the nurses. "Do you understand that it's the Secretary of the Army?"

"I DO NOT CARE."

I didn't want to see my wife, my mom, Edward, or my brothers. I did not want to see anyone (and clearly now I couldn't), and I made that abundantly clear. *Leave me alone. Just leave me alone and let me be blind.* And then someone knocked on the door of room 5831 and waited for me to answer.

A nurse told me that it was a boy—probably about ten years old. Tiffany walked to the door and came back to my bed. "Scotty, it is Andrew from West Point—Andrew Harris."

I didn't answer right away. I panicked. *Andrew Harris from my Sunday school class? I haven't seen him for two years. He used to look up to me. I used to make him laugh. Now I'm just a blind guy lying here and he is going to think I am pathetic. How can I be his hero?* "Who is Andrew

Harris?" I said out loud. I knew who it was, but I didn't want it to be him. I was scared.

Growing up at the United States Military Academy, Andrew Harris had thousands of role models to choose from. I could see in his face that cadets were what Andrew liked most about the years at West Point. "I got to see them every day," he told me much later. Andrew and I formed a great bond the moment we met in Sunday school class. His mom told me that he loved coming on Sunday mornings because he knew when he got there he was going to get to spend some time with me. Relationships like that made it easier to get out of my West Point bed on the weekend. "Dreeewwww," I would yell down the caverns of Thayer Hall as adults shuffled their kids into classrooms and stared at me disapprovingly.

And when I yelled his name, Andrew Harris at eight years old would light up like a firefly on a summer night. "My name is Andrew, but you always called me 'Drew.' You're the only person who ever called me that," Andrew later shared, "but I liked it. It made me feel special." A winter-sports-loving army brat with tightly cropped hair, Andrew found in other cadets and in me people whom he could look up to—as men, as Christians, and as servants of something bigger than self.

The last time Andrew remembers seeing me—and the last time I saw Drew—was on Mother's Day of 2003. The Cadet Chapel hosted a picnic on Constitution Island, a small rock just across the Hudson River from the academy grounds and the place where the song "Jesus Loves Me" was written. The Harrises spent time with me that day, and Andrew remembers it quite well, because he recalls how sad he felt that we were going to be together for the last time. "I was really hoping to see you on graduation day, but with all of the crowds and cadets, I never found you."

I still wasn't really sure what I looked like, how ugly the scar on my head was, how steep the slope of my skull, or how sunken my eyes. Words formed on my lips: "Andrew Harris? I don't want to see him either." But I could not bring myself to say it. At the same time, I couldn't gather the courage to welcome him in. I was in the middle of a valley, suffering from intense doubt, and in my mind Andrew was still an innocent second-grader. He did not need to be interacting with me. I cried as I processed the depth of my self-loathing.

But Andrew and his dad had driven five hours from West Point. I wondered how they even knew I was injured. And as I wondered that, I felt my first spark of self-confidence since the injury. How did they know? And why did they care? They really drove all that way to see *me*? Wow. Maybe my wife still cared about me. Maybe my family and friends were surrounding me because they wanted to, and not just because of my sorry state.

I assume that Andrew stood patiently, suffering in silence as I processed my self-absorbed thoughts. I made him wait there for close to ten minutes. Andrew told me later on that he had no idea what to expect. He wondered how I would look. He even wondered for a second if I would remember him.

"Hi, Drew. Come on in."

Andrew walked in and apparently my appearance did startle him a bit. He knew from the prayer request he'd heard at the Cadet Chapel (that's how he found out) that my injury had been severe, but he didn't know just how bad it was until he saw me lying there with tubes growing from my limbs. As a result of the craniotomy, the slope of my head resembled Mount Rainier. As a result of the recent surgeries, my eyes made me look like a zombie. Fuzzy growth covered my face—evidence of my indifference. My bed was in the back left corner of my room. When people came in, and especially when Drew came in, I wanted to hide the left side of my head, the misshapen side. But I couldn't, not with my bed in the position it was in—my left side was in full view. *Why couldn't I have been on the other side of the room?*

"I was shocked when I saw you," Andrew admitted later. "I wanted to cry, but I didn't. I didn't because I would have been embarrassed to cry in front of you." Little did Drew know I had been crying as he waited outside my hospital door.

I hadn't wanted to see Toby Keith, or Gary Sinise, or an anonymous civilian official from my chain of command (although I appreciate now the time they took to visit the hospital). But I raised within myself the guts to see Drew. And really, I couldn't not see him. I don't remember at all what we talked about—probably just about school and skiing and Drew's cross-country. But Andrew Harris's presence deflected thoughts of self and forced me to realize that I still had responsibilities to others—heroic-level responsibilities.

Maybe more important, Drew brought joy into the room. He smiled just as I always remembered him smiling. I couldn't see it anymore, his smile, but I could feel it. Back at West Point, kids like Drew used to be so happy to see me on Sunday mornings. They wanted to please me, and wanted me to praise them. In class, Drew's hand was always in the air. In second grade, he would fight through a tough-sounding verse in Corinthians just to hear me say: "Great job." And then he would smile a really big smile. I'd rub his head. He was such a cute kid. What surprised me most about the hospital visit was that in some ways it wasn't any different than on those Sundays at West Point. Drew was still smiling—with his voice this time—and he was still trying to please me. To him, I hadn't changed at all. I was still worth something.

As Drew left, I told him that someday, when he got to West Point, maybe he could be in my class. My fight to stay on active duty would ultimately continue for many more months and my dream of teaching leadership was not yet even a distant fantasy, but Andrew apparently smiled at the thought nonetheless.

I spent the hour after Andrew's departure reflecting on the permanence of my blindness. I remained depleted. I still didn't want to smile and didn't want to fake any emotion. But somewhere, a pin of hope: *Maybe there is still something special about me?* My wife, my parents, my siblings, and my closest friends were supposed to love me. People like Toby Keith wanted to stop by to be kind. But Andrew, he had come because he still thought I was cool, a role model, eyes or no yes.

At Walter Reed, I was constantly receiving medical updates. My blood pressure was stable. My brain swelling was down. I had almost fully recovered use of the right side of my body. A few hours after Andrew left, my brother Stephen walked in with another update. He put his hand on my right shoulder and said in a strangely serious voice: "Scotty, the doctors are concerned about your left-sided chest hair." I asked Stephen to repeat the concern.

"Your chest hair is not growing on the right side. The doctors are concerned that you are only going to have chest hair on your left side." Stephen was completely serious.

My reaction was visceral. I had no time to stop it. I smiled, and then I laughed. I told Stephen I thought I could get by in life with chest hair on just one side but that it would be great if they could fix it somehow.

God sent me two blessings that day. He sent me Andrew Harris, and he sent me a message about chest hair. One made me think about something other than myself, and one made me laugh, even if I hadn't wanted to. It was a brief moment of brightness. And in that moment, my gears started turning.

I sat up in my bed and declared: "I am going to take a shower."

Tiffany, who had returned to my side when Andrew left, freaked out (not about the chest hair but about the shower). "Scotty, sit back down," she pleaded. But I would not listen. Intravenous cords flapped around the room and a monitor followed behind me as its plug pulled me back toward the wall. I said with more force: "I am going to take a shower." *My eyes will not define me.*

I had no idea how large the room really was. Because there had been thirty people crammed in there at times, I figured it to be the size of a racquetball court. I expected the walk toward the shower, wherever the shower was, to be thirty or forty feet at least. Tiffany pushed me back toward the bed with one hand as she reached for the nurse alarm with the other. She pushed the button again and again, hoping someone would come help her contain her suddenly insane spouse.

I was rarely indignant, but the sugarcoated happiness of my own personal choir had grated on me. And when loved ones and friends weren't singing and dancing by my bed, the medical personnel stepped in and poked and prodded. Every six hours a new doctor or nurse would pepper me with questions about my mental awareness. Tiffany wondered why someone didn't just write down on my chart that I did, in fact, know who I was and where I was. Or that I understood I would have only half of my chest of hair!

"Where are you right now?" a nurse would ask me. The first eleven times I answered the question. On the twelfth try, I mixed it up.

"I am in West Palm Beach, and the ocean is beautiful."

The nurse widened her eyes and pressed on. "Okay then, Lieutenant Smiley. And what do you want to do in the future?"

"I want to be an airline pilot." *Stop treating me like a buffoon! I want them all to stop treating me like I'm completely lost.*

The singing, the questions, the darkness—it all made me want to roll off my bed, slide down a long dark tunnel, and splash into unconsciousness. But instead, I decided to do something normal.

"I am taking a shower!"

Tiffany's pleading turned to crying as my strength waned and my legs quivered. She told me she would get some help and kept pushing that alarm. But I did not want any help. I had taken thousands of showers by myself before. "Get out of my way," I told her. "I can do this by myself."

Nurses arrived just as Tiffany's spirit was breaking. They settled me into a wheelchair, despite my protests, and rolled me to the bathroom. I stripped my own clothes off as two women I did not know grabbed me underneath my arms and nudged me onto the cold tiles of a Walter Reed shower. "Watch out for the lip," said one of them. I stood there in darkness and grabbed for a handle. For the first time, it hit me that there was no use in reaching for a light switch. Feeling only flatness with my hands, I rotated 180 degrees and found a piece of metal. As I turned it counterclockwise, cold water sprayed down upon me. My legs, which hadn't done any work in well over two weeks, ached and shook as the lactic acid broke apart. The small indentions under the balls of my feet, where grout cast a border between one-inch tiles, stuck into my skin. I stood there motionless with my head drooping forward. I had no strength. I was pitiful.

The nurses took soap and sponge and washed dirt, sweat, and Iraqi garbage off my body. I moved slowly forward, as if I was going through a car wash, and then slowly turned around so that the water was splashing on my back. It felt awkward to be fully exposed in front of these two people. They could see me but I could not see them. It didn't seem fair. But I was glad to have them there washing me, because I could barely move my arms.

I had sworn to defend the Constitution. I signed up to give my life for my country. But my eyes? I *never* signed up to be blind. It was the most horrible shower I have ever taken: lonely, cold, and dark. But in a small way, it washed away some of my helplessness. I had gotten out of that bed and showered. One step forward in a journey with no end in sight. While I would discover that gutting it out in my own strength could only take me so far, for now I was more alive than I had been since I "woke up."

CHAPTER 16

HOLDING ON

I have been asked on hundreds of times in my life why God allows tragedy and suffering. I have to confess that I really do not know the answer totally, even to my own satisfaction. I have to accept, by faith, that God is sovereign, and He is a God of love and mercy and compassion in the midst of suffering.
Billy Graham, September 14, 2001

During what became my two months at Walter Reed, a vast and amazing network of family and friends came to support me. Edward Graham came. Dave Webb and Adam Rivette came. Therese Van Antwerp, Jeff's wife, came, along with Jeff's brother Luke. All my family and all Tiffany's family came. Kevin McDonnell was in and out every day, making sure the Thompson Twins had my care under control. Paula Van Antwerp—Jeff and Luke's mom—drove north from Fort Monroe, Virginia, the minute she heard about my injury. West Point classmates stopped by. Colonels and generals peeked in and mingled with my nephews and nieces.

Jeff Van Antwerp sacrificed almost the entire two weeks of his mid-tour leave to be with me, canceling a trip to the Caribbean with the blessing of his wife. Although to this day I feel guilty that Jeff altered his plans, Jeff assures me he didn't do it just for me. He soothed my guilt in the aftermath: "Scotty, you had all kinds of people around you. You didn't need me there. I did it for me. I needed to be there and to see that you were going to be okay. Yup, it was way more for me."

The peak of activity in my room took place two days after my cold shower. Just after noon, on the third Friday following my injury, a crowd stuffed itself into every corner of room 5831. To the right of my bed were General Farmer (the commanding general of Walter Reed), Lieutenant General Van Antwerp (Jeff's dad), my brother Neal, Neal's wife, Carrie, and their daughter Lauren, Tiffany's mom, Kevin McDonnell, John and Andrew Harris, and many others. Everyone had gathered for a Purple Heart ceremony. At first, I wondered who was receiving the Purple Heart. Whether because of the drugs or the emotional pain, my mind was not working at 100 percent.

At some point, as the room rustled to a quiet, it occurred to me that this ceremony was for me. I lay on my bed, faceup, in a forest green T-shirt. A thin line, where my head had been sliced open during the craniotomy, branched off from my forehead and traced through the center of my short, dark hair. Friends have described the rest of the scene to me as it had been played over and over again in a video that Luke Van Antwerp made. Tiffany stood over me to the right as Neal, wearing the army's old camouflage uniform, looked down at a citation that he held in his right hand. Neal opened his mouth. He paused and then gulped. His head bowed forward and then tilted back. And his lips spread apart once again.

"The President of the United States of America has awarded the Purple Heart . . ." Neal stalled, choking back unfamiliar tears. Tiffany claims that through all the pain, Neal's bravado had come in handy. He had been a constant encouragement. As others close to me struggled with their own emotions, Neal continued to assure Tiff that everything would be okay in the end. But despite Neal's positive attitude, the reading of my Purple Heart broke his stiff upper lip.

" . . . established by General George Washington . . ." Neal swallowed two more times and paused again.

" . . . in Newburgh, New York, 1782, is presented to First Lieutenant Scotty Michael Smiley, United States Army, for wounds received . . ." And the dam of Neal's voice broke. It was almost a relief to hear him let go and just water the moment with his emotion.

" . . . in action, on 6 April 2005."

This moment meant that it wasn't a dream. I could almost see the shrapnel flying at me, and I wanted to duck. But I couldn't. I couldn't get out of the way of this new life. Service to my country—this ceremony and this Purple Heart—meant that I had paid an expensive price. The war carried on, but I was no longer a part of it. I was a wounded vet, lying in a hospital bed. Again, I fought off feelings of worthlessness and despair. The shower no longer seemed like such a victory. It was, after all, only a shower.

"Given under my hand, this day, in the City of Washington. Signed, James Harvey, Secretary of the Army."

As Neal read, a single stream flowed from the corner of my right eye. I held my left arm up toward my head. At the level of my ear, my elbow bent ninety degrees and my forearm covered my face. I was embarrassed to be crying in front of everyone. Andrew Harris could see me now. Tiffany touched me, unable to do anything but just be there. My upper body convulsed and my mouth gaped. My moans mixed in with Neal's announcement. They were the only two sounds in the overflowing room.

Probably one of the only people on earth who could have brought brightness to my world stood next to Neal. General Van Antwerp—or

Van as he asks everyone to call him—is one of the most charismatic people on the planet. At six feet three and somewhere near sixty years old, he still has every strand of hair that he started life with. It's silver now, making him all the more distinguished. Van is Santa Claus without the beard or the belly. It's no surprise Jeff Van became the leader that he did. He was brought up by a father who simply gets it.

As the Purple Heart ceremony drew to a close, Van provided genuine encouragement that would, a few years later, ring prophetic. "I just hope and pray for your recovery," he said gently as his voice turned in my direction. He continued, "And we'll see what God has in store for you and Tiffany for the rest of your life. The one thing I know is that it's gonna be good . . . and it's gonna be exciting. And so, we're holding on here, and we're with you. God bless you, Scotty."

Tiffany tells me she nodded her head throughout Van's proclamation. I didn't move. I wanted to believe in those words—that there was some sort of plan and some sort of hope for the rest of my life—but I didn't see it yet. Still, whether I could receive what General Van was saying or not, that moment was not just about me. Van's encouragement lifted Tiffany up at a time when she needed it most.

"Lieutenant General Van was that beacon of hope," she said to me later. "He shined through the darkness and made me feel, once again, like it would all be okay. Not that you would see, but that you would believe. That we would have a life together, somehow. I just felt in that moment like, yes, you are going to be able to do things."

I still was not sure, and I would not be for a while. Once everyone poured out of the room, having congratulated me, it all hit home. I made a mental map of the road I had traveled to this location.

I was on patrol in Iraq.

A man with a fuzzy face and head raised his hands and then blew up his car.

The shrapnel destroyed my left eye and took the vision from my right one.

The doctors in Iraq removed a piece of my skull.

I went to Germany. My sister Mary Lynn met me there.

I flew back to the United States with Mary Lynn next to me.

I came to Walter Reed.

I woke up blind.

I had an operation.

I will never see again.

I took a shower.

I just received a Purple Heart.

Why, God? Why?

The weeks following the Purple Heart were filled with physical therapy. The bruising of my left frontal lobe warned of traumatic brain injury (TBI), so doctors took me through every single precaution, as if they were operating from Appendix A of *Basics of Neurosurgery.* As I slogged through walking exercises and muscle movements, I let my appearance deteriorate. *I can't see,* I figured, *so I don't care what I look like.*

When Jeff Van Antwerp visited, he scolded me and gave me a haircut. After the trim, Jeff took me down to the gym and challenged me to a pull-up contest. "I did twenty-something," remembers Jeff, "but you did eight or nine. You had been through a bombing in Iraq and spent the last month and a half in hospitals, and yet you knocked out nine pull-ups." Funny that Jeff praised me while still making it clear he smoked me.

The physical therapist glanced at Jeff as I raised my chin above the horizontal bar. When my feet hit the ground after my final repetition, the therapist exclaimed: "This guy's been sandbagging me." I hadn't, but Jeff's presence and support provided me some motivation.

I said that I didn't care what I looked like, but not all my actions supported that claim. The bane of my existence was an enormous green helmet that doctors ordered me to don every single time I left my bed. With that piece of my skull missing, only a soft stretch of flesh stood between my brain and the blunt and sharp objects of the world. The helmet, which could be described as half a watermelon, or something the New York Jets would have worn in ancient Troy, announced to everyone within a half of a mile that I was *different.* I wore it while at Walter Reed, but once I broke out of that place, I traded the Trojan hat for a baseball cap, risking my life every single minute rather than looking the fool. It was a theme that would become familiar in my new existence. Before leaving Walter Reed, I received a prosthetic left eye and a prosthetic cover for what was left of my right eye. I looked better, according to Tiff, but of course from the inside out, nothing was any different. Still, I guess I was glad I looked better.

Jeff Van Antwerp headed back to Iraq mostly confident that I would regain my fire, stand shoulder-to-shoulder with Tiffany, and conquer life. Jeff had too much faith, in the Lord and in me, to believe anything less. "This injury isn't bigger than God," Jeff proclaimed to me. I wasn't even close to sure. It was a pretty big injury.

PART III

BLIND WORLD

CHAPTER 17

LOST

For in hope we have been saved, but hope that is seen is not hope.
The apostle Paul, in his letter to the Romans (chapter 8, verse 24)

Two miles southeast of Stanford University, on the far side of Page Mill Road, sits Building 48 of the Veterans Affairs Palo Alto Health Care System. Building 48, which according to Tiffany has the pleasant look of a college dormitory, is the Blind Rehabilitation Center. A sidewalk circles the three-story structure; inside the perimeter of the sidewalk are grassy areas, one of which harbors a wooden picnic table, a horseshoes pit, and a putting green. Beyond the sidewalk is a vast network of parking lots, both cement and gravel. At the entryway to the entire V.A. complex flies an enormous American flag, big enough to parachute with.

Somehow, Tiffany and I have the strength to find comic relief in our Silicon Valley experience. My time at the Palo Alto V.A. came close to reconfiguring the me whom my friends once looked up to as the Oak. "I was amazed that you didn't go crazy," Tiffany said later. "To go from being a strong infantry officer, you know, leading your platoon in Iraq . . . to that situation? I was amazed that you humbly complied."

The Palo Alto V.A. was my first stop after Walter Reed, but before I began my actual blind rehab work, I spent a week at Building 7, working through mundane exercises in an attempt to prove that I did not have debilitating traumatic brain injury (TBI). From Sunday through Friday, I was trapped in a space no larger than a small apartment. The floor plan formed the letter *T*. A stretch of room ran, I would guess, about sixty feet and then met a hallway maybe thirty feet in length. "Do not leave this area," I was told, "or alarms will sound." *You have got to be kidding me. I walked in here by myself and now I'm a prisoner?*

One day the staff provided me an "exception to policy" and allowed me to eat outside with Tiffany. On a different afternoon, I received a pass to walk around the building. One lap took about five minutes. Tiffany and I laughed at the fact that I needed a pass to go on a five-minute walk. However, as I realized who was in the TBI department, things began to make a little more sense. I shared this experience with actual TBI victims, people who were eating through straws and could barely speak. All of the meals were ground or blended like baby food. People were seriously injured here, and the staff wanted to check my brain for damage. It made sense. But the experience was enough to put me pretty near the edge.

To asses my mental wherewithal, a medical professional presented me with figures of speech. "Don't count your chickens before the eggs hatch."

"So do you want the literal definition or the figurative definition?" I asked. The tester was not sure what I meant. I was talking over her head (figuratively speaking).

"Okay, well don't count your chickens before the eggs hatch means that before the eggs hatch, there's a possibility that one or more of the embryos could die. If that happened, you would end up with less chickens than eggs; so you don't want to count the chickens before the eggs hatch." I provided a similar explanation for "People who live in glass houses shouldn't throw stones" and eight other examples. I and my literal explanations failed miserably. The woman came back the next day and gave me a multiple choice test. This time, the figures of speech had figurative answers. I scored ten out of ten. The woman compiled my results and explained to me that I had some trouble with nonliteral language.

When I pressed the tester for a way to cure my mental ills, she seemed amazed that I was actually interested in getting better. She opened a file cabinet and took out a page of exercises for me to work through. I could not read it—I'm blind—but with Tiff reading it to me, I smoked through it in five minutes. Once Tiffany and I had completed my language exercise, I hugged her in jest, jumped up and down, and yelped: "I'm cured! I'm cured!" It was funny and it wasn't.

The laughter provided Tiffany a temporary release from the strain of her crumbling identity. It created a familiar scene in her brain—the two of us joking together and making fun of a ridiculous situation. On our honeymoon, during a few hours when I took a break from windsurfing, we had boarded a glass-bottom boat for a three-hour tour of the Jamaican underworld. The boat was rustic and authentic, so authentic that the wood seats suffered from peeling paint and splintering boards. In an effort to protect the fine buttocks of my new bride, I stepped up to the front of the boat and secured a life vest, one of those giant orange horseshoes that slip around the back of your neck.

"Here, Tiff," I joked aloud as I lowered the life vest onto the wood seat. "This should protect your hemorrhoids from the splinters." Tiffany glanced left over the rail of the boat, thought about jumping, and glared at me. I looked around at the other passengers. And then I laughed. And then she laughed.

Tiffany was the only family member with me in Building 7 and later in Building 48. Social workers continually pressed her to go home and tend to the rest of her family. Tiffany told them that she wasn't going anywhere; she might as well have had her hands wrapped around my legs like a kid holding on to her mother. A kind staff member felt compassion for Tiff and would sometimes bring her another patient's leftover food. Every night, she left Building 7 and walked to a hotel down the street.

"I didn't care. I was going to be there no matter what," she told me. "I just didn't see leaving you as a healthy thing to do. You needed me there." It was a surreal and disorienting experience for both of us. All we had as a lifeline to anything we had known before was each other.

On the day of my transfer out of Building 7, the TBI personnel put me in a wheelchair to roll me over to Building 48. I cringed with embarrassment; my right-side paralysis had worn off, and I had been walking for weeks. I fought with the nurses, but they wore me down with arguments about my own safety. Tiffany told me to sit down and let it go. When a rolling version of my blind self arrived at the rehabilitation center in Building 48, the nurse greeted me with a question. "Okay, sir, so are you always in a wheelchair?"

I stood up proudly. "No. I'm fine. I don't know why they made me sit in this thing."

Before my move to Building 48, I received an update from Tiffany. "I saw some blind people today," she told me.

"Really?" I responded with curiosity. "What did they look like?"

"Well, I don't think they were really blind," Tiffany confided, as if these people were committing some sort of crime. "They had their walking sticks, but they weren't using them. They just carried them six inches above the ground. They were chitchatting and talking like nothing was wrong at all."

Tiffany had stumbled onto an unlikely fact—once I arrived at Building 48, we learned I was the only blind person in the Blind Rehabilitation Center. I was not the only person. I was the only *blind* person. And I was at least thirty years younger than any of the other people. My fellow patients suffered from cataracts, loss of peripheral vision, blind spots in their sight, and numerous other afflictions. But none was 100 percent blind.

I had to stay at the rehab center full-time. I couldn't leave and go sleep at the hotel with Tiffany. I was in a bare-bones room with an AM/FM radio, a bed, and a sink. They set the alarms to wake us up at five-thirty every morning so the seniors could go get their coffee.

At breakfast, I used my walking stick for its intended purpose. I'd walk into the mess hall, take a right, and head to the second table, second seat in. A lady with supposedly crazy and colorful hats sat on my left. Across the table was a Vietnam vet who routinely bragged about his drunken assaults of military police officers and adventures at brothels in Saigon. The Vietnam vet drove his car to the V.A. and parked it across the street so no one would catch him. During breaks in rehab, he would evade the staff and fit in exhilarating joyrides. One day he showed up at lunch and said that he could see. Apparently an operation had corrected his vision impairment, so he walked to his car and drove home. Tiffany and I are not sure how he drove before the operation.

To my left was a piano player named Tom. He was barely five feet tall, but his tickling of the ivories went all the way back to World War II, when he used to entertain crowds of servicemen in French cafés. Sixty-plus years after the war, Tom would hold concerts in the Building 48 lounge. The other patients stood around singing and clapping. They all loved the place. They would tell me how the blind center had changed their lives. Some of them didn't want to leave. It was funny, but it wasn't. Deep down, I was scared. I didn't want to end up like any of these people. Perhaps that is a prideful, insensitive thing to say, but it is how I felt at that moment, unsure where my life was heading or what it was about.

Back at Walter Reed, I had struggled to maintain my dignity. One doctor had me count change for hours, testing me on the differences between pennies, nickels, dimes, and quarters. I would lower my hand to the table, feel for the coins, and then add up the total in my head. "Two quarters, a dime, and a penny—that is sixty-one cents," I announced.

"Well done, Lieutenant Smiley. Now try this combination."

I'm Ranger and scuba qualified. I dodged flying bullets. I wanted to pick up the change and hurl it across the room.

On another occasion, a physical therapist took me into what felt like a small closet. At one end of the closet was a set of bowling pins—Fisher Price bowling pins. The therapist handed me a plastic, weightless ball and told me to roll it to the other end. The clatter of tumbling plastic told me I had rolled on target. I then walked ten feet to the other side of the closet, set the pins back up, and rolled again.

Being subjected to these kinds of exercises was difficult to bear, but at least at Walter Reed I'd been surrounded by friends and family. Painful as it had been emotionally, familiar voices and personalities kept me grounded. In Palo Alto, I clung to the cliff of my own self-concept. Tiffany often raged inside at the way I was being treated. I imagine the staff members were selfless and dedicated, just trying to do their jobs. But this was not a place I ever thought I would be—in a dark corner of California, learning how to live without the benefit of sight.

In Building 48 they made me weave baskets and build crafts. I planed wood, cut it, and routered it. I felt fortunate to escape with all my fingers. I made myself a leather belt and a cane holder. I spray-painted things and sewed. *I didn't do any of these things when I could see. Why am I doing them now? Do they want me to be a belt maker for the rest of my life?*

For an entire week, a man put me in a car, drove twenty minutes, and then told me to walk around the block. I walked the square lap, and the man told me, "Good job." When I got in the car to head back to Building 48, I had to yell "Hands clear!" and raise my arms up before I was permitted to shut the door. After I made my pronouncement, the driver would repeat my refrain. "Hands clear," I shouted. "Hands clear," repeated the man. On the third day, I asked why I had to yell "Hands clear."

"It's just a good idea," he explained. "This one time I shut my hands in the door."

But you can see? Why don't you just get your hands out of the door?

I made a flower out of a piece of copper. I had to rub it with sticks, and I had to get each subsequent stick right. A woman's paid job was to watch me rub the sticks on the copper.

Building 23 was the gym. A good left fielder could have thrown a baseball through its front door from the back side of Building 48. Exiting the double doors, I walked about twenty feet, hit a black mat, and took a left. The sidewalk carried me fifty yards or so to another mat. A right turn and a quick left put me at the front door of the gym. Those hundred yards or so were my independence. Working out was a way to be who I was.

The gym smelled of chlorine, like the intramural pool in Arvin Gym at West Point. It was a quick walk from the gym's entrance to the double doors of the basketball court. Lining the walls of the basketball court were 1980s-era workout benches. I used my hands to feel the bars and the metal cables. As my hands touched the equipment, my brain processed the shapes. *Bench press. Incline press. Lateral pull-down.* On one occasion I felt an unfamiliar, circular machine. I moved my hands downward from the solid, scratchy surface until I felt the softness of skin. *That's a nose.* Someone was looking up at me. I could only wonder what they were thinking. "Sorry," I said as I moved on to the next machine.

I worked out for forty minutes that day. Then I walked back out into the chlorine-filled hallway and headed for the exit. As I've already shared, somewhere along the sidewalk leading to the door of the blind center, my stick missed a mat. Once I was off my known path, nothing could pull me back. I had no way to regain my bearings. For some reason—an act of rebellion, really—I stepped off the sidewalk, further disorienting myself. The next thing I knew, I was lost in that scorching-hot parking lot.

I struggled for half an hour and then dropped into a lump on the ground and began to sob. I had no idea who I was or where I was. Was I even a lieutenant in the army? I certainly wasn't a leader anymore. I felt like I was in some warped social experiment. My entire world had disappeared and been replaced with a joke. I asked God to tell me how I was supposed to take care of my family if I couldn't even walk back from the gym. I was tired of basket weaving and Tom's piano playing and being treated like a fool. *God, what do You want from me?*

I resented the theft of my dreams—my hopes of becoming a Fortune 500 CEO, or a Delta Force operator, or a four-star general. Instead, I was a grown man who needed help walking across the street. Coming out of West Point and Ranger School, I didn't exactly have my life planned out, but I had options. *And now I can't even walk back from the gym?* I wanted to scream, but all I could do was cry. I was so incredibly helpless sitting there in that moment, hot, lost, and disabled.

What do you want from me, God? Why am I even alive?

Oddly, almost instantaneously, I realized that I had never really committed myself fully to God's plans. I'd had *my* dreams and *my* plans and my own selfish pride. I had known God and believed in Him. I had prayed and tried to love and serve others. I had asked God to help me with my life's decisions. But I had never fully depended on God or hoped completely in Him. In some way, without realizing it, I had hoped in myself. I had relied on myself, on my gifts, instincts, and natural abilities. Those gifts and abilities had brought me a long way, all the way to the corner of Route Tampa and Route Porsche. But they could take me no further.

I had lost my way a while back—my inability to navigate had nothing to do with my eyes and everything to do with my lack of focus on what our finite time on earth is all about. I paused. I stopped crying. It occurred to me that if I was not capable of directing myself between two buildings—a left and then a mat and then a right—then what was I going to do with the big things? "Scotty," God seemed to be saying to my heart, "humble yourself and depend on Me." As I sat on that sidewalk I understood with clarity that hardships must occur for people to open up their eyes and see that they are really fools. If that's not true for all people, then at least for me that was the case.

God continued to work on my heart. "You are not this guy who can just do things on his own. You never really were. No one is."

I thought about Jesus. God's own Son needed assistance at the toughest moments of His life. When Jesus fell under the weight of the cross, a man came out from the crowd and carried it for Him. Paul had Timothy. Paul told the Philippians he could do all things, not by himself, but *through Christ* who strengthens. The me who could see was used to climbing mountains and thanking God for coming along. The me who could not see was totally dependent. "You need to trust Me, Scotty," I sensed God telling me "And you need to depend on others."

I can do all things. There is nothing in the Bible that qualifies that statement, nothing that says I need eyes. It says only that I need Christ. It was a truth that my blindness was going to help me see. My confidence was being moved away from self—from my own ability to see and control—to a new hope, a hope unseen.

The Smiley boys on Christmas 2009. (L-R) Neal, me, Stephen, and Nick. (Photo by Tiffany Smiley)

(L-R) Adam Rivette, Dave Webb, Edward Graham, and me in New York City during our final year at West Point. (Photo courtesy of Dave Webb)

(L-R) Kristy (Webb) Graham, Edward Graham, me, and Tiffany at Ranger School graduation, Fort Benning, Georgia. (Photo courtesy of Kristy Graham)

Tiffany and me at Edward and Kristy's wedding—shortly after Ranger School.

Dave Webb and me on the parade field at Fort Lewis, Washington—just prior to our deployment to Iraq. (Photo courtesy of Jeff Van Antwerp)

Captain Jeff Van Antwerp and me in Iraq, sometime around February of 2005. We were handing out free gasoline to Iraqis. (Photo courtesy of Jeff Van Antwerp)

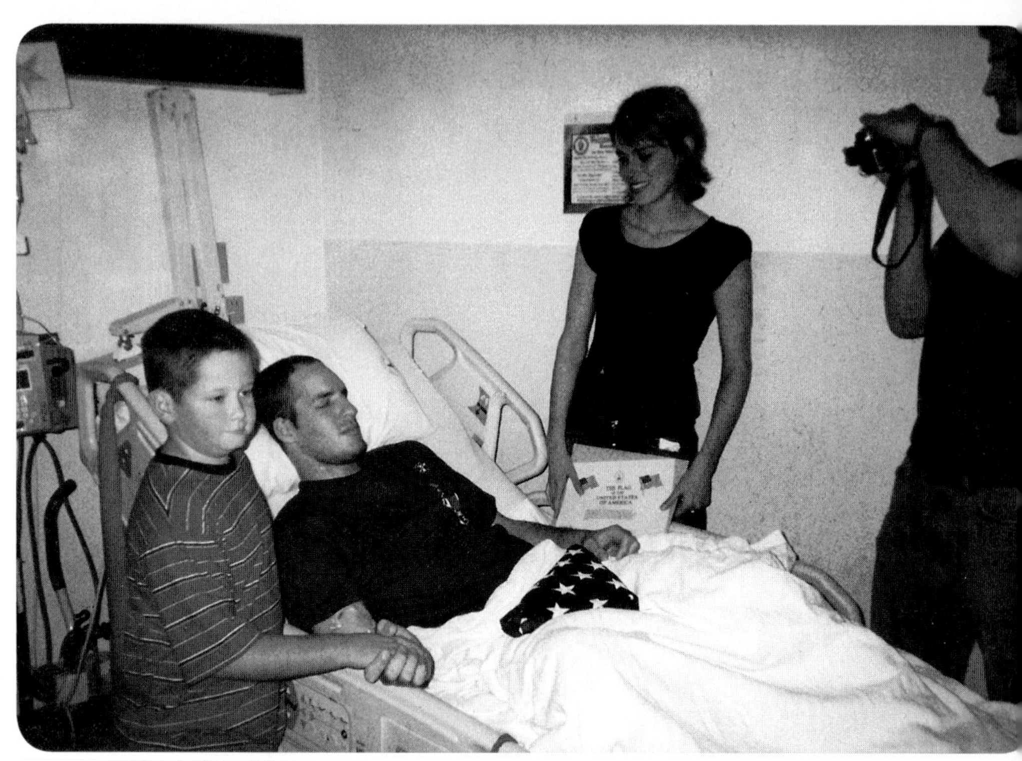

This picture was taken in my room at Walter Reed, shortly after I received the Purple Heart. Andrew Harris is the one holding my hand. (Photo by Karen Elliott)

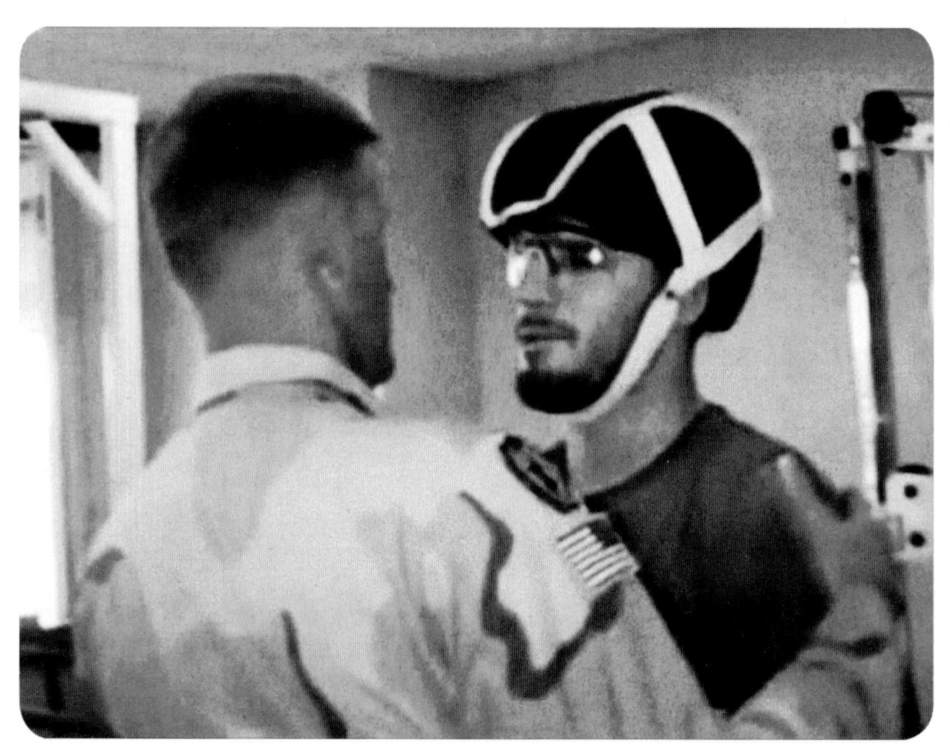

Jeff Van Antwerp provides me words of encouragement at Walter Reed. As you can see, my protecti green helmet was quite conspicuous. (Photo courtesy of Luke Van Antwerp)

Jeff and me on the North Shore of Oahu. A beautiful picture, from what I am told. (Photo by Peter King)

Paddling to catch the wave on my second day surfing—at Chun's Reef. (Photo by Peter King)

Getting up on a surfboard was an amazing feeling—something that helped me feel like I would be able to live life even without my eyes. (Photo by Peter King)

The best thing about surfing—just seven months after I had lost my eyesight—was the affirmation of my family and friends. I love the touch of my wife. (Photo by Peter King)

Climbing Mt. Rainier with Curtis Fawley as my guide.
Every step was grueling. (Photo by Gabe Rogel)

Tandem sky-diving with the Army's Golden Knights was one of the exhilarating opportunities that came my way in the wake of my injury. (Photo courtesy of the Golden Knights)

Tiffany, Grady, and me at the Duke versus Navy football game.
I helped the Blue Devils with the coin toss. Beat Navy!

My first lesson teaching leadership at West Point.
(Photo by Amanda Miller)

(L-R) Graham, me, Grady, and Tiffa
People tell me that my children are
beautiful. Unfortunately, I just can'
picture them—but I am thankful for
the life God has blessed me with.
(Photo by Amanda Miller)

CHAPTER 18

NORTH SHORE

It's like in the great stories, Mr. Frodo, the ones that really mattered. Full of darkness and danger they were, and sometimes you didn't want to know the end because how could the end be happy? How could the world go back to the way it was when so much bad had happened? But in the end it's only a passing thing this shadow, even darkness must pass. A new day will come, and when the sun shines it'll shine out the clearer.
Sam Gamgee in *Lord of the Rings: The Two Towers*

On Halloween of 2005, doctors crafted a silicone bone implant and fused it to the rest of my skull, covering up the frontal lobe gap that I'd been walking around with for nearly six months. They didn't end up using the preserved bone that had been in my abdomen since the surgery in Iraq. That type of replacement surgery had been an air force convention. Army doctors preferred an artificial skull section.

Three weeks after my surgery, Tiffany and I trekked to Hawaii to stay with friends—actually, with the family of Dave Webb's wife, Tanya. Years earlier, Jeff and Luke Van Antwerp had rented an apartment in Hawaii. They attended church with Tanya Bridgman's family, and Dave met Tanya there during the summer before our final year at West Point.

Tanya's family is North Shore royalty. Scott Bridgman, Tanya's dad, arrived on Oahu in 1972 for a two-month vacation and never left. He married Miki, an Oahu native. The couple purchased a two-story house one cul-de-sac over from the Pacific Ocean. They surfed almost daily—big waves, small waves, whatever the ocean provided. They raised four daughters. Their girls, with flexible home-school schedules, surfed daily as well.

Over the years, the Bridgman home became a resting place for transient wave seekers. Each month, dozens of twenty-somethings would climb the wooden stairs to the Bridgman Inn, let themselves in the deck door, take a shower, and crash on the couch. Some of them were attracted to the hospitality; others were attracted to Tanya and her sisters; and some of them just needed a place to lay their heads.

Tiffany says the Bridgman home looks as if it had been designed for the very purpose of lodging surfers. An older wooden stairway climbs up to a second-floor deck. Under the outside deck are thirty-some surfboards in all shapes and sizes. Walking up those stairs, I felt a strong fear of splinters. The railings hadn't been sanded and refinished in a while. At the top of the stairs is a rickety screen door where shoes and sandals are piled—a hazard for a blind person. When I took my shoes off and left them in the pile, I could feel the scratch of sand underneath my feet. The sandy entrance opens to a great room with three big couches. The couches are laid out in a U-shape—something I figured out on my own—so all of the visitors can talk to one another.

In the process of providing food, shelter, and sunscreen for myriad vagabonds, the Bridgmans became the hub of North Shore surf life. They knew just about everyone who had paddled a long board out toward the local waves.

On our trip after my surgery, Tiffany and I took up residence with the Bridgmans. Arriving on the island and feeling the warm sun on the back of my neck, I felt some disappointment. I recalled the tropical lushness of our Jamaican honeymoon and longed to look around at the Hawaiian scenery. But I fought once again, as I had in Palo Alto and as I would for years to come, to see hope in the darkness. *This blindness is the life God has blessed me with, and it is something I have to live with and even grow to love. I am on Oahu and I am lucky to be here.* Instead of my eyes taking photographs of the green hills, blue skies, and tranquil waters, I settled for Tiffany's nondescript, even lame, oratory.

"Well, it's really sunny out." Tiffany had not signed up to be a tour guide for a guy who couldn't see. A few years later, I would come to realize that Tiff also stank at television play-by-play.

"Michael is wearing women's clothes and Darrel is making fun of him," Tiffany would say.

"Okay, I got that part," I retorted, "but who else is laughing at him?"

The scene had already changed, and Tiffany couldn't remember the blond girl's name or who else had been standing there. "No one else was around, just Pam and Dwight."

"Tiffany, I know that other people were around. Who was it?"

"Just listen to the show, Scotty."

"You stink at this, Tiffany. How am I supposed to watch *The Office* if you don't even pay attention?"

Sitting on the U-shaped couch at the Bridgmans', I wasted no time getting to know Tanya's father, Scott. "I heard that you're a great surfing teacher," I brown nosed as Mr. Bridgman braced for the inevitable. "Will you take me surfing?"

Mr. Bridgman remarked a few years later that he thought I was dreaming—crazy even. In his mind, surfing in the bathtub was too big a risk for a blind man. He was not going to take me. But before Mr. Bridgman even had time to respond, I spewed out more desire. "Yeah, because, I've just got to surf Pipe."

Pipeline, as it is known more formally, boasts some of the biggest waves in the world. During November and December, the barrels can reach twenty feet high. Pipe is home to strict surfing etiquette, a distinct pecking order, and it attracts the sport's best surfers. Scott Bridgman had just met me. I'm sure he had no idea what to say, but he mustered this tactful response. "People die trying to take on Pipe every year. The waves are enormous. Scotty, *I* don't even surf Pipe."

"Sir," I countered, "I am scuba qualified. I am a lifeguard. Sir, I am trained to do dangerous things." Scott Bridgman just looked at me (I'm guessing—maybe he looked away in embarrassment). In his heart, he later told me, Mr. Bridgman appreciated my enthusiasm and zest for life. But zest didn't mean surfing in Hawaii—not on Scott Bridgman's watch. His thirty years of North Shore experience told him that it was not a good idea.

As I remember it, Mr. Bridgman mentioned the danger I would pose to myself and to others, and although Scott Bridgman is too nice a person to have ever intended it this way, I took the concerns and denial as a personal rejection, an indication that a blind guy was not capable and should not be daring such mighty things. I figured I would have to get used to a lot of that. *For the rest of my life, people will doubt me and tell me what I can't do* (even if their hearts are in the right place). I decided I would calmly but decidedly prove every single one of them wrong.

I moved to another couch and sat next to the deck door. I distracted myself with conversation as I tabled my surfing dreams for the moment. It's weird. Sometimes I care what the colors surrounding me are and other times I don't. I could tell that the couch I was sitting on was older, but it was soft and extremely comfortable. I felt like I was in the middle of a giant marshmallow. There were so many other things to explore in the Bridgman home—noises, the taste of salt in the air, the smell of pineapple—that I never asked about the colors. But when I do wonder, I've learned to just speak out loud: "Hey, what color is that wall over there?" "What kind of television is that? How big is it?" The Bridgmans' walls were mostly white. The staircase was made of dark wood, and the television was a flat-screen—about forty-six inches.

As people wandered in and out of the Bridgman home, I would hold out my hand, open up my smile, and announce: "I'm Scotty Smiley, who are you?" I met countless surfers, talking to each of them about the waves in the ocean and the waves of life, all the time never giving up on the idea of conquering the North Shore. (Scott Bridgman had, however, convinced me that, eyes or no eyes, I would die if I tried to surf Pipe.)

One of the first opportunities I had to share my story was at North Shore Christian Fellowship while on that trip to Oahu. I was so nervous. I have never liked public speaking, even when I could see. It makes me sick to my stomach to this day. I worry that I will forget what to say. At Ranger School, I couldn't even remember the creed. Back at West Point, in our first-year poetry class, we had to memorize an entire poem. I practiced for three days, got up in front of the class, recited four stanzas, and drew a blank. The teacher shook his head and told me to sit down.

Even if I do remember what to say, I worry nobody will care, or that they won't understand the message. Because I can't see people's facial expressions anymore, I have no idea whether I am boring them to death, making them angry, or making them cry. I imagine they are making fun of me while I speak. I even worry sometimes that people will think I deserved to be injured, that I shouldn't have been over there, fighting *that* war. It may seem irrational, but it's my reality.

So why do I speak? I speak because I believe God has called me to share my story as a help to others in difficult times. I overcome my fear in the hope that my pain will help ease someone else's and that the triumphs God has given me will inspire others. Selfishly, I speak because it helps me heal.

I was just beginning to learn how to share my story when Tiffany and I were in Hawaii with the Bridgmans. As the pastor of North Shore Christian Fellowship introduced me to the church, I wanted to run out the back door. *Why am I doing this?* Once he turned it over to me, I stood still and bawled for a good seven minutes (seriously). But after I sniffed away my emotions, I tried to echo Lieutenant General Van Antwerp's Walter Reed declaration: "I'm not sure what God is going to do with my life, but I know that there are good things in store and that He has a purpose for me."

The Bridgmans' next-door neighbors, the Woodring family, sat in on the service that day. They had a connection to what I shared. When their son Cole was two, he suffered a terrible eye injury. He had chased his aunt out the front door while carrying an oddly shaped picture frame. The frame had a wire coat hanger twisting up from its top right corner. Cole's parents had scolded him for carrying the picture frame around the house. They'd set it up on a shelf where he couldn't reach it, but Cole was fascinated by the shapes. When his parents weren't looking, he monkeyed his way up some furniture and grabbed it. He liked the frame so much that he wanted to show it to his aunt. Running on to the porch, focused on the silhouette of his mom's sister, Cole Woodring missed the six-inch drop from his front deck to the rust-colored cement step below. His left knee buckled and his head lunged forward. The coat hanger plunged into his right eye, ripping apart his cornea and the lens.

For seven years, doctors would battle to save Cole's right eye. Toward the end of the struggle, in the winter of 2009, Cole spent two straight weeks facedown on a massage table with his head peeking through a twelve-by-twelve-inch square. Any movement, even minor, risked damaging a repaired retina, so his parents strapped him down at night and monitored him all day long. He watched a television that sat on the ground and read books from his horizontal position. For a nine-year-old boy, the immobility was the worst form of torture. Eventually, Cole's parents decided that the debilitation of the continuing medical onslaught was not worth it. Cole is now legally blind in that right eye but free to roam around as he pleases.

Cole Woodring is a scrappy little guy with glasses, brown hair, and a don't-mess-with-me sense of humor. He hounds his parents to play baseball while touting his domination on the soccer field. Speaking at North Shore was a huge struggle for me, but when I connected with the Woodrings, I realized God was using my injury somehow to bring a bit of peace to other people's lives. Cole, like Andrew Harris, looked up to me and helped me see that I still had something to offer.

By mid-November, seven months after my injury, my battalion had returned to Fort Lewis. A few weeks later, Dave Webb and Jeff and

Therese Van Antwerp joined Tiffany and me in Hawaii. I wasted no time. "Jeff, you're a pretty good surfer. Will you take me out?"

"Pretty good surfer?" Jeff retorted with a laugh. "I am an awesome surfer. Of course I will take you out surfing, Scotty."

Jeff Van Antwerp would have done anything for me, and I would do anything for him. What was important to me right then was that Jeff didn't have the grown-up caution of Scott Bridgman. As Dave, Tiffany, Tanya, and Therese shook their heads in silence, Jeff and I walked downstairs to the underside of the Bridgman deck and grabbed two boards. Just like that, I was in business.

Jeff took me to Haleiwa Beach, not quite Pipe but still the North Shore of Oahu. Paddling out through Hawaii's ocean waves at midday resembles chasing a sparkler on the Fourth of July. Bright spots of sun reflect off the water and sting the eyes. The surfboard bounces up and down with the waves. On the uptick the expansive horizon is plainly in sight; on the downslope a wall of blue stares you in the face. The surfing area at Haleiwa Beach falls just outside a small cove formed by a wall of rocks on the right and an open area of calm on the left. The average surfer with two good eyes will point his board toward the end of the left-side rocks and paddle through the twinkling light and the ups and downs until he is beyond the cove.

I simply followed Jeff's voice. I didn't see any sparklers, and the bank of rocks meant nothing to me. Cold water splashed in my face and every once in a while, the familiar taste of salt reminded me of Jamaica. As I bounced up and down with the waves, the sudden movements caused my body to slide along the rough traction material attached to the surfboard. The sandpaper-type stuff removed a few hairs from my chest (which was now growing, as normal, on both sides). I was both comfortable and cold at the same time. Goose bumps broke out on my legs, but the sunshine warmed my back.

After about fifteen minutes, I was exhausted. The paddling stuff was hard, and I just had to trust that Jeff knew where we were going. Left arm circle; right arm circle. I felt as if Mr. Miyagi from *The Karate Kid* were watching me and laughing. Thirty total minutes of arching my back and holding my neck up made my entire torso ache. My arms hung off my body like pieces of soaking-wet wood. During the swim, I realized I did not need to hold my head up, as I had nothing to look at. I am blind. This made the paddling a little bit easier, and I continued on with my head down. Having traveled out to the point where Jeff was waiting for me, I turned my board back toward the shore. Jeff gave me brief instructions on sprint-paddling when the right set came. "Stand up when you feel it." *Feel what? What is he talking about? Thanks, Jeff.*

When the next set rolled in, Jeff began to push on my board. "Paddle, Scotty! Paddle!" I threw my arms in and out of the water, trying to create the momentum Jeff had described. I could feel the waves approaching behind me, and I accelerated my revolutions. The waves passed by, but I never felt *it.* All I felt was a bunch of water rushing over the back of my legs. I was now thirty yards closer to shore and thirty yards farther away from Jeff. I'd have to play Marco Polo with Jeff to get back out and try again. The pain in my limbs, neck, and back urged me to quit. I thought about it, but I was done with quitting. I could do this. I turned my board back around and paddled toward the sound of Jeff's voice. *Oh, this stinks,* I thought to myself.

A few minutes later, it was time to try again. Jeff pushed the back of my board and yelled at me to paddle. This time, I gained a sense for the speed of the approaching wave. I anticipated that moment at which I would feel it. *Here it comes. Here it comes. Now!*

I gripped the front of my board with both hands and pushed my chest away from the fiberglass and sandpaper. As my upper body leapt skyward, I bent my knees and flipped my feet forward. They landed on the center of the board just as the wave caught up. The breeze in my face and the absence of salt water in my mouth told me that I was actually standing. It was like riding a roller coaster in the dark. I had no idea what was out in front of me or when I was going to stop. But eyes or no eyes, I was engaged in life. I rode that wave for seventy-five yards, my arms outstretched for balance and my hair blowing in the wind. Had I been a complete loser, I would have yelled: "I'm the king of the world!" If you've never surfed, you might not know how hard it can be get up on a board. I had tried for days to find my balance windsurfing in Jamaica, and I never did it. In Hawaii, with no eyes, I got up on my second try. I do believe God was holding me up that day, showing me in small ways that He could be trusted—that I could do surprising things if I would just depend on Him.

When I felt the board slowing down, I jumped off into the water. From a distance I could hear Jeff cheering for me and yelling at me to paddle back out and try again. A large dose of adrenaline soothed the aches that the paddling had inflicted. *Surfing is awesome!* I raced back out toward Jeff's voice and reloaded. Five times that day I surfed the waves at Haleiwa. It was a beginner's ride for your average sighted person. It was a triumph for me. I was so proud of myself. I had been lost at several points during the previous six months, and I'd had many struggles. But I was learning that if I believed in myself, asked God for help, and reached out to others, I could overcome my limitations. And I did it.

Jeff was maybe the only guy at the beach park who knew I was riding toward the shore, unable to see a thing. He told me there were perfectly healthy young people with professional coaches who still were not able to get up on their boards that day. As we packed up and headed home, Jeff summed up the situation pretty well. "I guess when you have trusted God with your whole life, trusting someone to get you on a wave is no big deal, huh?"

When we returned to the Bridgmans', Jeff announced the results to the entire group. Tanya, Dave, and Therese were in shock. They had seen hundreds of people come to the North Shore, declare their intentions to surf, and come back to the house defeated. It hadn't crossed their minds that I would actually succeed in riding a wave. Tiffany snuggled up against me, ignoring the cold of my wet shorts, and whispered in my ear: "I'm so proud of you, Scotty. I love you."

When Scott Bridgman returned home, I didn't waste any time. The little kid in me kicked in. "Jeff and I went surfing today at Haleiwa."

"Seriously?" queried Mr. Bridgman, not yet willing to believe. I know he must have looked around the room to check others' faces for some type of reassurance.

"Yeah," I replied. "It wasn't that hard." It was that hard, but Mr. Bridgman didn't need to know that. Not right then.

A day later, Scott Bridgman drove by Chun's Reef on his way home from a contracting job. In terms of difficulty, Chun's is a step up from Haleiwa Beach. But that day, the surf appeared calm, just tiny waves toppling in toward the shore. Scott told me that he looked out his driver-side window and decided: *I can take a blind guy surfing in that.* He drove home, parked his truck in the driveway, climbed the stairs, and called me. "Get over here now and I'll take you surfing at Chun's Reef."

A member of North Shore Christian Fellowship who had just been certified as a lifeguard was hanging out at the house. Eavesdropping on Scott's conversation, he figured out what was going on. "Hey," he interrupted, "I'll come out there and help." The pieces were falling into place: perfect waves, empty waters, and a lifeguard for safety. Mr. Bridgman planned to take me out there and just let me swim around a little bit—success at Haleiwa or not, he didn't figure I would catch a wave at Chun's.

Two hours later, we finally made it to the beach. Everyone was there with me this time. But suddenly I could tell that Scott wanted to back out. While he'd been assembling the operation, the waves had grown from one or two feet to four or five feet—fairly large for a blind surfing novice. But there was no way I was turning back. "Just lead me out there," I said to Scott, "and I'll make it happen."

Joining Dave, Jeff, Tanya, Tiffany, and Therese on the beach that day was a professional photographer who regularly freelanced for Hurley surf gear. The photographer just happened to be shooting at Chun's; he had no idea when he woke up that morning that we'd be out there.

I was an expert surfer in my own mind at this point. I followed Scott out to the starting point just as I had followed Jeff Van the day before. Just like the day before, I felt the wave, transitioned to my feet, and surfed some waves. The photographer was there to catch it all in still frame—anyone who didn't believe me could see it in black and white.

It was awesome to feel the ocean underneath my board, to feel alive and be alive. But surfing is not what stood out to me that day. My clearest memory is of the love and respect I gained from Tiffany and others on that island. I felt the warmth of so many amazing relationships that God has blessed me with. I knew that many tough times lay ahead in my life, but there in Hawaii I was learning how to trust God for help. In small, incremental ways, I was beginning to live in the truth of that promise, "I can do all things through Christ," whether all things meant standing up and speaking (or crying) in front of a crowd or just getting up on a surfboard.

Embracing on the beach at Chun's Reef, Tiffany and I had no idea where we were headed. The army was still pursuing my retirement. Waiting back at Fort Lewis was a whole new evaluation process, poised to turn me into a civilian. Back in Washington, D.C., Lieutenant General Van Antwerp had told Tiffany: "If this happens again, just give me a call. Just give me a call and I'll take care of it." Jeff Van had taken me surfing. His dad was now poised to help us tackle the next challenge—staying in the army.

Chapter 19

HOME OCEAN

A dog doesn't care if you're rich or poor, educated or illiterate, clever or dull. Give him your heart and he will give you his.
John Grogan, *Marley and Me*

On any given day back in Washington, Tiffany bought in moderation with an understanding that a lieutenant's salary didn't make us rich. But on Oahu? As I had learned while deployed to Iraq, Oahu crushed Tiffany's will to resist. As she strolled down a crowded sidewalk on a warm summer day in Honolulu, the gravitational pull of every passing store forced Tiffany to admit her weakness. In our relationship, Tiffany's often the strong one. No officer in the army had quite ever held Tiffany Elliott–type power over me. And yet Tiff turns into a little girl when she knows she is spending too much. Her look turns bashful and the whisper in her voice communicates her guilt. So as we ventured into the heart of Waikiki, I reminded her that *I* was making the financial decisions. No three-hundred-dollar dresses or two-hundred-dollar pairs of shoes. I didn't want to argue about it. Since we didn't have that kind of money, I just asked Tiff to listen to me about the budget stuff.

With early-morning shopping scratched from the agenda, we opted for some breakfast. Tiffany picked out a reasonably priced café, and we enjoyed time together as our Hawaiian adventure drew to a close. Blindness makes the simplest of tasks adventurous. I can't read a restaurant bill or even sign my name in the right spot without help. Tiffany read me the total: toast, eggs, and juice added up to just over sixteen dollars. She asked me what she should leave as a tip. Feeling generous, I told Tiffany to just give the server twenty.

Maybe Tiffany was upset that I would give a tip of over three dollars, or maybe she was just curious, but a few minutes after we left the restaurant she interrupted whatever else we were talking about and said: "Wow, Scotty, that waitress did a good job, huh? You sure gave her a big tip." I was kind of proud of my generosity, but just over 20 percent wasn't that much, especially considering the small cost of the breakfast.

"Well, it was just three bucks. I didn't think it was that big of a deal."

"Three dollars?" queried Tiffany. "You told me to give her twenty."

"Yes," I said, "I told you to give her twenty dollars for the whole bill."

"Scotty, you told me to give her twenty. I gave her a twenty-dollar tip. I thought it sounded like a lot, but you told me not to hassle you about financial stuff, so I didn't."

"Holy smokes," I exclaimed. Then I started laughing nervously, hoping Tiffany was just joking. When I realized it wasn't a joke, my prosthetic eyes nearly popped out of their sockets. After a long conversation about finances, we had just tipped a server in Waikiki close to 125 percent.

Our marriage relationship, our friendship, had always been pretty balanced. I wasn't trying to control the money necessarily, but I did have a deep need to feel worthwhile. Maybe I had the whole money conversation because, given how dependent I was on Tiffany, I needed to be giving something to who we were together. I could be the responsible financial partner even if I couldn't see. Surfing in Hawaii provided me an incredible thrill and gave me encouragement that I would not have to spend my life sitting around on the couch, but I was not going to become a professional surfer, and day-to-day, darkness still prevailed.

My need for purpose grew more desperate when we returned to Fort Lewis. Mundane routines engulfed my existence. The army assigned me to a medical hold company, and my only real responsibility was to make it on time to doctor appointments. I tried to spend time working out with Jeff Van and other guys from Alpha Company, but when the weightlifting and running were over, they had jobs to do, and I went back to the house and sat around. I don't want pity, but just close your eyes for an hour and sit in your living room. It gets boring pretty quick. Now imagine that's the rest of your life and you're not sure when you will have another chance to surf.

Within a couple of weeks after the return from Hawaii, my sleep patterns deteriorated. Some nights I would do okay, but other nights I would lay awake for hours, thinking about the nothingness of the next day. Meanwhile, the army was still pursuing my discharge. This time, it was the Fort Lewis system in gear, preparing the paperwork for a medical evaluation board that would assess my fitness for service. Had it not been for the help of Colonel Kevin McDonnell and the Thompson Twins—and for Tiffany's prescience in refusing to sign those papers—I would have been deemed unfit back at Walter Reed. I could feel the tug of time dragging us closer to that verdict at

Lewis, and the thought of even less meaning—the thought of losing the army role that I loved—terrified me. I tried to trust that God had it all figured out.

On the outside, I portrayed joy. I couldn't bear to make others' lives miserable. Therese and Paula Van Antwerp told me it was amazing how I never seemed to have a down day. They figured that the normality of daily life, in the wake of the hospitals and the vacations and the surfing, would crush my spirit. Wouldn't I break down and cease to function, they wondered, the moment I realized I couldn't drive my wife to the movies? Or when it became clear that everyone else was going back to work and that I wasn't?

I was feeling some of those things. I just didn't let it show on the outside. And as much as it was a struggle, I prayed constantly and read the Bible (well, I listened to it), turning to God to carry me through the whole mess.

Tiffany and I had done some research online and talked to some friends, and multiple people told us that a four-legged companion would soothe some of my feelings of isolation and worthlessness. I could raise a dog, feed a dog, walk a dog, and care for a dog. The dog would need me, which is what I needed. So on a dreary winter day, I jumped in the Chevy Tahoe with Tiffany and Taylor Van Antwerp (Jeff and Therese's daughter) and rode north to Renton, Washington. Rain dumped on our heads as we slogged through the muddy backyard of a suburban house. The owner led us to a handful of yellow labs, all yapping with ferocity as we approached. Taylor loved the puppies; they barked and barked as they leapt onto her legs with their outstretched front paws. When Taylor knelt, I imagined the entire litter lunging at her face, attempting to lick her cheeks and earn some return affection.

I felt a tremor of annoyance shoot through my gut. Purpose or no purpose, the last thing I wanted was some yapping, pottying dog that licked me all over the place. I could hear Taylor giggling a few feet away, and I envisioned the swarm of puppies fighting for her attention. I really didn't want any of them and decided that this had been a bad idea. Tiffany just stood by with one hand on my arm and one eye on Taylor. About ready to ditch the rain and get back to the car, I felt a puppy rubbing against the bottom part of my leg. The puppy wasn't jumping or barking. She simply nestled her midsection just above the top of my shoe and stood there patiently, requesting my friendship.

"This one," I announced. "I want this one." I pointed toward my toes, hoping that the snuggling puppy was still in the proximity of my right foot.

Two hours later we were back at Fort Lewis with a new dog. We named her Ocean, after the surfing and the trip to Hawaii, which I already missed so much. Ocean became a quick friend, and while training her to go to the bathroom outside didn't involve the tactical, interpersonal, or cultural complexity of leading a platoon in Iraq, it did give me something to do. There is no doubt that I needed Ocean.

She was an ultraloving dog. When I walked in the door, I could hear her wagging tail slapping against the closet door. Even if I had been gone for just a few minutes, Ocean was happy to see me. Other than Tiffany, she seemed like the only creature on earth happy to see me. I needed Ocean to like me—being loved by her provided me a kind of emotional warmth that had disappeared from my life when I left my platoon mates. I would often grab Ocean by the midsection, pull her toward me, and just hold her in my arms, strumming her soft fur with my fingers, charting her growth with my sense of touch and perception of her increasing weight.

And yet, though Ocean provided me companionship and distraction, she did nothing to mend my sleepless nights. As the anniversary of my blindness crept toward nine months, I lay awake in bed one night, once again thinking about nothing in particular. It was somewhere around 2 A.M. I was tired of being tired. Tired of not sleeping, and tired of being blind. It was one of those moments—like the rush to the shower at Walter Reed, like the step off the sidewalk in Palo Alto—when I realized I was going to have to do something. Right then I had a wild hair. I decided to be Scotty.

I arose from bed, clawed through the night to find my pants and shoes as Tiffany slept silently, and then I summoned Ocean. The puppy pitter-pattered across the floor and rubbed her wet nose on my palm. I fumbled in the dark—it's always dark for me—until I found the leash, which was hanging on the coatrack. I reached back down, mapped my hand to Ocean's neck, and clipped on the leash. With the leash secure, I turned back to the coatrack and found my walking stick resting in the corner, next to the door. Just like that, with my stick our only guide, Ocean and I ventured out on a late-night walk.

About twenty steps beyond the front door, I felt the driveway end. I turned right and nestled my stick up against the curb. I had been on this walk before and knew I could circle the block in my Fort Lewis housing area without a problem. The outer edge of the sidewalk would be my guide, carrying me about forty yards forward, then right for thirty, right for another eighty, another right for thirty, and then a right for forty more back to our driveway. Except that Ocean didn't like the linear direction of my travel. She pulled me to the left, jerking the stick off the cement. I tried to get Ocean under control, but handling a puppy and a stick at the same time was the stuff of professional blind men. I was still an amateur.

Before my stick had even identified the first right turn, I felt a raindrop. And then I felt another. Within thirty seconds, rain pounded the pavement, as it always does in western Washington, and made its way down my face. I tasted some water and decided I should turn around. Ocean found the surrounding wetness to be pure terror. She began to scurry back and forth, and I just about lost control of my otherwise docile puppy. There was something about water that horrified Ocean. When I gave her a bath, she would freak out, shake, scamper around the tub, and try to escape over the porcelain wall to the freedom and sanity of dryness. It was as if she imagined water to be some sort of deadly acid, capable of melting her as it melted the Wicked Witch of the West. Ocean's irrational fear of wetness (which didn't go away until months later) wasn't doing me any favors as the rain picked up.

With one big lunge left, Ocean pulled me away from the curb; my stick dropped and we were lost. I could almost see the people at the Blind Center shaking their finger at me: "Lieutenant Smiley, we told you not to go out in the street." Life's options seemed limited: lie in bed in silence and darkness or get lost outside in the rain with a strong-willed puppy.

Again. Here I am again. I had learned from experience. Well, in one sense, if I had learned from experience, I wouldn't have been in this predicament. But once in it, I had learned that I could get out of it. I didn't break down and cry, not in front of Ocean at least. We were both lost, and I needed to get us home. It felt like Palo Alto (the rain notwithstanding), but it was different—pathetic but less desperate. I bent down on one knee, placed my hand on the coarse, wet ground, and felt for my stick. I picked it up and reoriented myself to the curb. "Home, Ocean," I commanded, almost laughing at the ridiculous words. Ocean had barely learned to pee outside, much less figure out what "home" meant.

We wandered for a bit in I don't know which direction. I had no idea which way I was even facing, just that I was tracing the outline of the curb. My emergency plan had been to listen for the sounds of Interstate 5 to the south, gain my bearing, and wander generally northward until I found a familiar landmark. But the loud rain drowned out the sounds of passing cars. Ocean and I shuffled maybe five feet as my dog sniffed and frolicked. Once more, I sent forth a Hail Mary command: "Home, Ocean." This time, Ocean seemed to get it. At least, she understood that I was asking her for something, even if she wasn't totally clear what that something was. Right away, she began to walk with more purpose, bouncing left and right some, but mostly taking a straight path.

As Ocean picked up some speed, I soon found myself trotting—fresh, shallow puddles splashing under me as my feet moved to keep pace with my dog. After a brief journey, Ocean stopped—and then she turned left and pulled me onto some grass. I sensed that I was in a front yard, and hoped that it was my own. I took the reins back from Ocean and pulled her to the left, stretching my right arm out in front of me as I felt for the shell of a car. Inching forward and grasping at air, my hand eventually ran into a large piece of metal. It was some sort of SUV or truck with windows and a roof at or above my eye level. I ran my hand toward the front of the vehicle until I bumped into a rearview mirror. It sure felt like a Chevy Tahoe.

The outline of a large vehicle wasn't enough for me to open the front door and enter a house. I was partly afraid of being shot, but probably more afraid of looking like an idiot. So I followed along the hood of the car until I felt a headlight. I pushed myself forward, reaching out for the back of a carport while Ocean pulled to the right. Once I found the back wall, I took a right and followed it to a doorknob. To the left of the door, about shoulder high, was a sign. I traced the letters *Merry Christmas.* I thanked Tiffany that she was a month late taking the decorations down, and then I stepped inside.

"Good girl, Ocean."

Chapter 20

CONNECTED DOTS

Jenny, I don't know if Momma was right or if,
if it's Lieutenant Dan. I don't know if we each have a destiny,
or if we're all just floating around accidental-like on a breeze,
but I, I think maybe it's both.
Forrest Gump

My fight for a life that consisted of more than waking, eating, and returning to bed began with tasks of excruciating simplicity. To communicate on a computer, I had to abandon a mouse and learn every single shortcut combination that a keyboard will allow. Small plastic dots on the F4, Insert, Alt, and Tab squares expedite shortcuts. Pressing Function and F4 at the same time closes an open window. The Ctrl key when combined with the U key underlines text in Microsoft Word. I poured hours per day into learning the new tricks that would gain me at least a modicum of independence.

A computer program called Jaws became one of my best new friends. In a *Star Wars*–type voice, Jaws reads everything it sees on a computer: e-mails from Tiffany, PowerPoint slides, file names, Internet advertisements. As my proficiency in understanding the robotic intonations of Jaws took shape, I increased the reading speed to twice the words per minute of a teenage girl talking on a cell phone.

Some people can't believe that even without the distraction of sight I can keep up with Jaws. But I do. I have to. I spent days upon days upon days in the winter of 2006 mastering the technology that would help me through the rest of my life.

A decision about my future in the army drew closer as winter wore on. On a Tuesday morning in March I headed to Madigan Army Medical Center for my first appointment in a new medical evaluation process. The army had restarted my retirement proceedings when I returned to Fort Lewis from Palo Alto. While I didn't want to exit the army, I tried to carry on without letting it eat at me. But what I could kind of stand, Tiffany could not. She felt like people were constantly doubting me. For the next three years, Tiffany would struggle with the naysaying of others.

From where Tiffany and I lived on the north side of Fort Lewis, the quickest trip to the hospital took us out the gate, up Interstate 5 one exit, off the freeway, and then into the Madigan parking lot. Getting into the parking lot meant passing through a security gate. While we waited in a line of cars, I asked Tiffany if she had seen my black beret (my army headgear). Out of half a million soldiers, at least several hundred thousand engage in a daily struggle to keep track of their berets. Throw complete darkness into the mix, and it's a wonder I ever had anything to put on my head. "I haven't seen it, Scotty," quipped Tiffany, annoyed that timekeeping, ironing, meal making, and now beret tracking were all on her shoulders.

While my right hand patted the passenger side floor in a hapless search for the feeling of brushed wool, Tiffany's annoyance turned into guilt. She twisted her torso counterclockwise and turned her head to look at the backseat: no beret. As she rotated her body back to the front and leaned over to look on the passenger side next to the armrest, Tiffany's right foot came off the brake.

Our Chevy Tahoe rolled forward while Tiffany was focused on the beret. Nine feet later, we knocked into the bumper of the car in front of us. Tiffany's head surged forward and her ear caught the radio. I had been sitting there oblivious—no passing trees or changing horizon to inform me that we had been rolling forward. I never felt the motion until we smacked the other car.

Tiffany recovered, pulled our Tahoe off to the side of the road, and exhaled as she looked at the rear bumper of the victimized car. There was an enormous dent in the back right fender, and the back quarter panel apparently looked like a crumpled piece of paper. The damage was probably in the thousands of dollars—all because of my beret and my inability to find it.

"I'm sorry. I'm sorry," Tiffany gasped to the other driver. She held back tears, she told me, wondering when life would start to get on her side. After a call to USAA and an exchange of information with the other party, Tiffany and I continued through the security gate and on to the hospital. There wasn't much time to worry about deductibles and future premium increases; Tiffany and I were focused on the evaluation board.

I walked across the Madigan parking lot without my beret. I held Tiffany's arm as I stepped up onto the sidewalk and proceeded toward the front doors. Just outside the entrance, under the cover of a cement overhang, we stopped to pray. We asked God to guide our future and to allow us to stay in the army if that was His will, but to care for and love us regardless of any specific plans.

Despite a surface of calm, I began to feel the same tremors of fear that had already been shaking Tiffany's world. *What am I going to do if I can't serve my country?* Hadn't I been here too many times before, wondering if God would take care of us? Life was by no means easy, but I'd already come so far since that shower at Walter Reed. At every step, God had provided. When would I start believing that He had things under control, even if my blindness didn't make sense to me? Did I hope in a purpose bigger than this world, or didn't I? Did I trust that if God wanted me in the army, there was nothing the evaluation board could do to stop Him? Did I trust that if He didn't want me in the army, He had a plan that maybe I didn't understand? *I did trust. I did.* God would provide—what I needed, if not necessarily what I wanted.

Tiffany and I sat squeamishly on a bench in the Madigan waiting area and prepared to reengage in the retirement process. Doctors would likely shine lights into my eyes, take some X-rays, and maybe even administer a CAT scan. They'd fill out some paperwork, ask Tiffany to sign in several places, and then, if we used common sense as our guide, likely declare that a total inability to see meant I should be a civilian. We had been able to delay this process to some degree since the day Tiffany refused to sign release papers at Walter Reed, but this time it would be harder to run away. Fort Lewis was our home, our permanent station. The army would just keep pursuing. On some level I understood. I mean, I was blind, and our army exists to fight and win our nation's wars.

"Lieutenant Smiley," a nurse called. She stood in the doorway leading back to the exam rooms. We walked over to the nurse and followed her back to what I think was yet another small, square hospital space. After the normal routine—blood pressure, temperature, and pleasantries—a medical board administrator walked in. "I'm sorry," he said, "but we are not going to be able to do anything today. They'll have to take care of you in Virginia."

Without the benefit of facial expressions and other visual cues, it takes me a while to digest confusing information. I often remain quiet longer than the average person as my brain churns through the things I have only heard with my ears. Tiffany, on the other hand, quickly shook off her surprise and asked the administrator what he was talking about.

"Fort Monroe—I've been told that you are moving to Fort Monroe. Some general called and had you reassigned there immediately."

My darkness notwithstanding, I understood. I quickly registered that General Van Antwerp had worked some three-star magic. Certain professional favors reek of favoritism. To me, Lieutenant General Van's care and concern smelled more like divine intervention. Even if not a direct answer to prayer, or an answer to prayer at all, this particular twist pointed to a tapestry of interconnected relationships and circumstances that I believe God provided in order to care for us: Jeff Van just happened to have been my company commander at the time of my injury. My sister Mary Lynn just happened to be in Germany as I hung on to life there. Mary Lynn's high school friend happened to serve at the air force base where I stopped. Colonel Kevin McDonnell happened to know the right people at Walter Reed. Now, when we needed it most, a three-star general happened to make a phone call at the right time. It helped me to review these events and connect the dots. In difficult moments, I could look back and encourage myself that God really did seem to be guiding our lives. That He did have a plan. That He loved us and had not forgotten us.

Comforting us further, a week or so later more good news arrived when Tiffany received word from an insurance representative at USAA. Apparently, the dent on the right rear of that car we hit heading into Madigan was not our doing—someone else had caused the damage in an earlier accident. To our great relief, fixing that car was not our responsibility. We were off the hook.

Chapter 21

SPEAKING OPPORTUNITIES

A successful person is one who is living a joyful life with the hand he or she was dealt.
Ron Hall, *Same Kind of Different as Me*

The initial six or so hours of our trip from Washington to Virginia were pretty happy. We moved east on I-84 without incident, chomping down Doritos and tossing water bottles and gum wrappers on the ground (we weren't mixing the gum and Doritos). My brother Stephen had volunteered to take Tiffany and me to Virginia, which was incredibly generous of him. We needed the help, because I couldn't do much driving and Tiffany was sick. Aside from the joys of having a personal chauffeur, riding shotgun gave me a chance to spend some good time with my big brother. He was a captive audience for my sometimes babbling rants.

But somewhere just east of Boise, Stephen too started to feel ill. "That dog is making me sick," he said between sneezes. I didn't know how a canine, especially one stuck in a tiny kennel in the back of the Tahoe, could be responsible for Stephen's inflamed nasal cavities and sore throat, but my older brother was blaming those things on Ocean.

I laughed with a little bit of choke mixed in. "Stephen," I retorted, "that's impossible. I've never heard of a dog transmitting a cold to a human being. Tiffany, you are a nurse. Is that possible? Could Ocean have made Stephen sick?"

Tiffany played Switzerland. She wasn't intervening in this argument (even though she knew I was right). For most of our trip, she had slept soundly, stretched out across the second-row bench with her legs bent at the knees and her head nestled on a pillow. I could hear her sniffling and imagined the rashes that had formed under her nose from all the rubbing.

With Stephen not in the mood for conversation and Tiffany zonked out for most of the forty-four-hour trip east, I sat upright in the passenger seat and bobbed my head to the sounds of Lifehouse and the Dave Matthews Band. I didn't get to see the Great Salt Lake or the wall of mountains to its east. When Denver rolled around, the weather turned bad, and an early spring snowstorm shut I-70 down for over two hours.

Unhappy with Ocean, unhappy with the snow, and generally unhappy with his now prolonged driving experience, Stephen shut off the music. I didn't feel like arguing, so I just sat there, in the dark, in the stillness. I could hear Stephen breathing, and I could feel the warmth of the heater blowing on my face from the right vent. I could hear the occasional rustling of Tiffany, and every once in a while a frustrated driver would honk his or her car horn. When I could focus my mind, I imagined the state of our Tahoe—food in all the cracks and fog covering the inside of all the glass surfaces. Had I been a kid (who could see), I would have played Tic-Tac-Toe with myself on the passenger window, but unable to compete against myself in an unwinnable game, I just sat. It was like being in solitary confinement.

With severe weather bringing traffic to a dead stop in the western part of Kansas, Stephen sought alternate routes. He navigated the back roads of the Midwest, thinking that the trip would be more bearable as long as we were moving. At one point, Tiffany asked him to stop the car. She opened the door, stepped out into the bluster, and puked over the side of a guardrail into a deep canyon. Then she got back in and Stephen kept driving.

Stephen and I had held our bladders and bowel movements in a sort of manly competition until one of us (Stephen as I remember it) eventually gave in and requested a stop. Ocean, however, never even tried to compete with us. The long, quiet drive was too much for my puppy; she pooped in the corner of her kennel somewhere east of Denver. Returning to a vehicle that had been dog-pooped in was almost more than we could take. But we didn't have too many options. Tiffany was sick. I couldn't drive. And we were in a rest stop parking lot in the middle of America. Stephen plugged his already stuffy nose, took a seat, and slotted the key into the ignition.

The weather, the dog, and the sickness notwithstanding, Stephen had a servant's heart. He was understandably frustrated at times, but he loved me with every ounce. Stephen had spent hours by my side at Walter Reed. He'd read me Bible verses, slept by my side, and prayed for my recovery. He means the world to me for all he did then and for all he continues to do. This miserable cross-country trek was just another demonstration of Stephen's true kinship, a testament to how much he loves me, and an example of the ways in which so many people have helped Tiffany and me.

We stopped in Nashville, where a relieved Stephen stopped for us to spend some time with our brother Neal and his family. Given Stephen's help through the first couple of thousand miles, Tiffany and

I were able to make it the rest of the way to Virginia by ourselves (and with Ocean, of course).

Tiffany and I traveled to Fort Monroe without any real sense of what I would be doing there. The move was better than the alternative—separation from the army—but it was still a reminder that our lives were kind of twisting in the wind. Of course, I was starting to believe more and more that the twisting had some direction—that God was leading me somewhere good, just as General Van had declared during my Purple Heart ceremony. Months later, I would realize I owed General Van more than I could have imagined. He had essentially created a role for me in order to keep me going in the army—a role that provided Tiffany the time to discern our next steps.

That's not to say I didn't earn my money while serving in Virginia. Lieutenant General Van Antwerp put me to work as a public speaker. As the director of U.S. Army Accessions Command, General Van ran everything from marketing to recruiting to the in-processing of new recruits. He sent me out to address soldiers, prospective soldiers, the influencers of prospective soldiers (parents), and key strategic partners in the army's endeavor to fill its ranks. There were two potential messages that people could take away from my story: (1) join the army and you too can lose your eyesight in the Middle East, or (2) join the army, serve your country, and become a person who demonstrates optimism and determination in the face of challenges. General Van trusted that people would glean the latter.

For the next year, Tiffany and I would travel throughout the States, speaking to military audiences and church communities. Monday through Friday I shared my commitment to the army and to our nation. Every time I spoke, I healed. I would still get nervous in front of audiences I could not see, but I started to have a greater sense of purpose in my life as I interacted with others. My speeches—and my continued service on active duty—were giving others hope and helping the army in a small way. I felt like I was contributing again rather than just taking from others.

The weekdays took me to military venues. On Sundays I shared about the ways I was growing in God through my recovery. I had the opportunity to speak at churches across the country. Each time, I cried a little less than I had at North Shore Christian Fellowship, and I processed emotions I hadn't yet had the desire to reflect upon. As I worked and contributed, my life started to gain some meaning. And some really great opportunities came my way. I was invited to ski in Vail (for me, every slope was a double black diamond) and skydive with the Army Black Knights parachute team. These adventures built on my surfing experience, and with each one, I gained more boldness and the courage to live with all my strength.

In the summer of 2006, Coach Mike Krzyzewski invited another wounded warrior and me to speak to Team USA basketball: Dwight Howard, LeBron James, Dwyane Wade, Carmelo Anthony, Shane Battier, and the rest of the national team players and coaches.

Colonel Bob Brown, who had been my brigade commander in Iraq and played basketball for Coach K. at West Point, put together the opportunity. He was the one who introduced me to the team. He rose from a chair to polite applause and stood in front of a group that, collectively, had made hundreds of millions of dollars during their playing careers.

"Selfless service," instructed Colonel Brown, "is what makes teams great. It's putting the needs of someone else before yourself. And on the basketball court that may be diving for the loose ball or taking a charge; on the battlefield it may mean running into a wall of bullets or putting your life on the line for someone else—to that level of selfless service."

I sat behind Colonel Brown with my eyelids jumping as I listened to a speech whose punch line was me. It was hard to believe that I was sitting in a small room with the U. S. Olympic basketball team. Not only was it hard to believe, it was deeply humbling. All I had done was lose my eyesight on the street in Mosul. What really gave me the privilege of spending some time with these athletes?

"So Scotty Smiley," continued the colonel, "he saved a lot of lives, 'cause he stayed up and fired. And when the bomb exploded, he took a piece of shrapnel in the eyes. He doesn't have any eyes. It looks like his eyes are normal, but he does not have any eyes." It was true that I didn't have eyes. I wasn't sure if it was true that I saved a lot of lives. I had done my job—led from the front—but it was just a car bomb. I did not deserve any really special recognition from Colonel Brown or this team. But there I was. Really, all I could believe was that God must have wanted me there, in that spot, on that day, to share my story.

Sitting across from me in that hotel conference room decorated in deep shades of red (I asked), the members of Team USA were pretty quiet. I wondered what they were thinking, even what expressions they were making. Colonel Brown paced in between the players and me. "He demonstrated selfless service in the lives he saved and in everything he's done, but he *fought* not to get out; he *fought* not to get out. I was over [in Iraq] fightin', and I got a call . . . that Scotty Smiley wants to stay in. They didn't know what to do. They'd never had a guy that was blind try to stay in. You know, come on, this doesn't make sense. He fought to stay in . . ."

Colonel Brown's voice trailed off with emotion. I choked up as well. "Sorry," the former Army basketball player apologized as he composed himself. I'd never known him to show emotion like this before.

"He's in," proclaimed Colonel Brown. "He's still serving. And as Scotty told me earlier, he's no different than before. He had problems before; he's got different problems now. That's a hero."

I am told that I received a standing ovation from the world's greatest basketball players and coaches. I was touched and not sure how to respond. I don't think I am a hero. I'm just trying to live my life and honor God. I could name some real heroes. But it did feel good to have those guys clapping for me—good in the sense that it helped me believe I was making a difference. I'd fought to stay in the army partly because I didn't know what I would do if they put me out. I still wanted to serve. Inspiring people, providing some sort of hope, felt like serving. In the end, those guys weren't clapping just for Lieutenant Smiley. They were clapping for everyone who has fought for our country. I could have come back from the war with both eyes, and I never would have had the opportunity to experience that kind of appreciation for our service men and women. I started to feel like my privileges were becoming a responsibility, and responsibility was something I welcomed back into my life.

After I shared my story and the meeting concluded, Tiffany and I had the chance to sit courtside for practice. Dwyane Wade and Gilbert Arenas provided commentary via a remote microphone, with the highlight coming when Carmelo Anthony put up a three and came away with an air ball. "Ooh, he must be tired," suggested Gilbert.

"Scotty, can you hear me?" Dwyane Wade was on the mike later in the session. I waved across the court to acknowledge his question. What he said next put words to what I felt earlier in the conference room as the players and coaches expressed their appreciation. I listened to Dwyane and was moved—moved on behalf of all the men and women who have committed themselves to service.

"Scotty," he said, "when we put these jerseys on, we feel a lot of pride walking around with 'USA' on our chests. I know you all got a lot of pride, and you guys are role models for a lot of us out here. We don't get a chance to tell you all, but you are role models for us, and we respect what you do for our country."

Chapter 22

ALMA MATER

And when our work is done,
Our course on earth is run,
May it be said, "Well Done;
Be Thou At Peace."
Paul S. Reinecke, "West Point Alma Mater"

During the summer of 2006 the army promoted me, along with the rest of the West Point class of 2003, to the rank of captain. At about that same time, Jeff Van Antwerp moved to West Point to begin an assignment as a cadet company tactical officer. Tiffany and I took several trips there to visit with Jeff and Therese. During our first trip, Jeff and a friend took me wakeboarding on Lake Popolopen. I had done quite a bit of wakeboarding while growing up near the Columbia River. Now that I was blind, my only fear was of the shore. I told Jeff to keep the boat at least twenty yards away from hard ground.

I could picture Lake Popolopen in my mind. It is located at Camp Buckner, where all West Point cadets spend the summer between their freshman and sophomore years. There would have been green trees all around, a couple of red wooden buildings, a small inlet with a dock, and a tiny, sandy beach. Popolopen's water was ice cold. I grabbed the handle on a ski rope as my life vest held me bobbing in the lake. I could hear the slight hum of Jeff's boat as he asked me if I was ready. I was.

"Hit it."

I popped up immediately and felt the wind in my face. This was much easier than surfing. In fact, the last time I had been wakeboarding I had been doing flips and one-eighties. This—wakeboarding—was something I was good at. My confidence swelled. After about thirty seconds of boarding (and worrying that Jeff was too close to shore), I shifted my weight and headed outside the wake to the right of the boat. I rode out there for a while and then cut back left to the middle. My board caught an edge, and I went crashing into the water. The left side of my head hit first. *Ouch. That hurt. What's wrong with me? Why can't I even cross back over the wake?*

Although my confidence was growing, wakeboarding demonstrated that my life clearly had limitations. My own personal balance between humility, confidence, independence, and dependence was still sorting itself out. God gives and God takes away. If wakeboarding was something He was taking away, that was okay.

We visited the Van Antwerps a couple of times that fall. In October, Doug Crandall, who would eventually become my coauthor, invited Jeff and me to his leadership class as guest speakers. We sat in front of fifteen cadets and talked about Captain Jacobsen's death, my blindness, and our relationship as commander and platoon leader. The topic for Doug's class that day was "Leading in Times of Trauma." The story I shared was similar to the one I had told on other occasions, but it felt different speaking with cadets. My story was relevant to them. They would be platoon leaders soon, out in front of Stryker formations. I had enjoyed the opportunities General

Van had provided me at Fort Monroe, but I really loved my time in that leadership class.

The thought of teaching at West Point as a full-time vocation went through my mind, but I quickly let the idea go. I didn't feel ready. My grades at West Point had been average. I didn't think I had enough army experience to be a valuable role model to future leaders. I had not commanded an army company—a standard requirement for officers who return to teach at West Point. Even if I shook off my own doubts and considered myself qualified, certainly West Point would not think of me as a good choice. I was just too inexperienced.

For a cadet, the best part of West Point is leaving—seeing Thayer Gate in the rearview mirror on graduation day. *Why would I want to go back?* First, I would have to go to graduate school, and I would have to take a standardized test in order to gain admission. The SAT tormented me when I had functional eyes; how would I possibly endure a GRE or GMAT now that I couldn't even see the questions?

Tiffany and I prayed about our future direction. My return to West Point for visits with Jeff and Therese had been oddly nostalgic. I couldn't see a thing while there, but then again, I could. I spent four years growing up at the academy. When our car for the first time turned down from Michie Stadium toward the Cadet Chapel, I knew where we were headed. I could picture the chapel rising above Eisenhower and MacArthur Barracks. I saw "the apron," the long stretch of concrete in between the barracks, and the grassy plain. Beyond the academy grounds, I envisioned the Hudson River. In my mind, winter memories of the Hudson were the most clear—when ice would float north to south in front of our classroom windows. Even though I couldn't see my surroundings, I had the sense of comfort that comes with being at home.

Before pouring my energy into the idea of returning to my alma mater in a teaching capacity of some kind, I had to figure out if it was even a remote possibility. As I said, I guessed it would be *very* remote. I floated the idea to the Van Antwerp family during a dinner at Fort Monroe. A couple of days later, Lieutenant General Van Antwerp called Brigadier General Patrick Finnegan, West Point's dean. Simultaneously, Jeff Van Antwerp mentioned the idea to Doug Crandall, who was then serving as the dean's executive officer. Major Crandall carried the notion across the hall to Brigadier General Finnegan. To my astonishment, it took General Finnegan seemingly little time to make a decision. The dean wanted me to come teach! I couldn't have been more surprised if I had woken up the next morning and seen Tiffany's freckles.

General Finnegan had been sitting in the back of the room when I visited Doug's leadership class with Jeff. For those fifty-five minutes, the dean saw me interact with cadets on a personal level, and given that "interview," he provided his stamp of approval. The fact that officers teach at the academy alongside dedicated civilian faculty members no doubt is part of the reason that the Princeton Review rated West Point the college with the "most accessible professors" and *Forbes* magazine rated it the number one college in the country. I was proud, overwhelmed, to think I might soon be one of those officers and that I might have the chance to invite cadets to my house, share a classroom with them, and work out with them in the mornings. Even though I was blinder than a bat, I was being given an opportunity to teach leadership at West Point—to guide a future Lee or Grant or MacArthur or Patton or Eisenhower or Schwarzkopf or Petraeus. *No way,* I thought. *This might really happen.*

Looking back, it was surreal to think that just eighteen months earlier, Tiffany had come a pen's stroke away from signing me into retirement. We were so thankful she had gone with her gut and, true to her strong-willed form, resisted that course. Now we were looking forward to a new chapter in my service career, one I would never have conceived outright. I was just walking out my journey one step at a time when my heart opened to West Point as a place where I longed to serve. In a way, it was as if I walked into an opportunity somehow designed for me. A late-November call from the dean himself, informing me that he wanted me to earn my M.B.A. and then come back to teach, launched me into a new stratosphere. I went from a guy who fought to stay on active duty to a person who actually had something to contribute.

Back at Fort Monroe, I ran down the hall to tell Lieutenant General Van. "Sir, you will never guess who just called me: Brigadier General Finnegan, the dean at West Point. He wants me to come teach." General Van smiled.

The journey through a life of blindness makes for a good story (I hope), but it doesn't earn you a red carpet walk into the nation's top M.B.A. programs. I set my sights on Stanford and Duke, preferring the latter if for no other reasons than a hesitation to return to Palo Alto, California, and a great friendship with Coach Mike Krzyzewski of Team USA, who coaches the Duke basketball team. The challenge was that by now the second-round admissions deadline was approaching rapidly at both institutions. I had applications to fill out, essays to write, and letters of recommendation to secure. Most important, I had to not only study for and succeed on the Graduate Management Admissions Test (GMAT) but to navigate a maze of bureaucracy to simply have the test administered.

I read through pages of literature on disabled test taking. There were standard accommodations for a number of nonstandard cases. Blind test taking came down to a case-by-case basis. Prove to us that you can't see, the instructions seemed to say, and we will go from there. The process for proving blindness could take up to eight weeks. I wondered why they couldn't just throw several footballs at me and watch them hit me in the stomach. But the Graduate Management Admissions Council (the GMAT bureaucrats) wanted a notarized letter from a doctor. Simple enough, except I was dealing with an army medical system that prioritized emergencies. An appointment to see the family physician might take a couple of weeks. I did not have a couple of weeks.

It really wasn't GMAC's fault that I was in such a hurry. The whole plan had come together in a moment. From Thanksgiving to the dean's decision to scheduling the GMAT, less than a week had transpired. Tiffany and I turned once again to God. He had been showing us what to do step by step, and we believed He would do the same now. If God wanted me to take the GMAT in time to apply for Stanford and Duke, then God would provide.

Meanwhile, Doug called Coach Krzyzewski to let him know of the dean's plans for me and to ask for a bit of assistance with the admissions team at Duke's business school. Coach K. called back and vowed to do whatever he could. While I waited for my paperwork to get to the right person at GMAC, I poured every extra minute into studying for the test. Tiffany was right there with me, reading out the questions and the multiple-choice options.

"Okay, Scotty, two travelers are trying to estimate their travel time by using a map. On the map, a distance of three centimeters represents an actual distance of forty-five kilometers. The distance between their initial location and their destination is fifty-five centimeters. How far will they have to travel?

"*(A)* six hundred kilometers. *(B)* seven hundred and fifty kilometers. *(C)* eight hundred and twenty-five kilometers. *(D)* nine hundred and twenty-five kilometers. *(E)* one thousand kilometers."

"Could you read the question one more time, Tiff?"

For hours upon hours, Tiffany read and I tried to process the questions, do the calculations, and remember the answers. According to www.gmattestquestions.com, the solution to the above problem is choice *C.* To get to that answer, a sighted person might convert forty-five kilometers to 450,000 centimeters in his head. But he might then turn to pen and paper and construct a ratio of 3 cm/450,000 cm = 55 cm/x, and use cross-multiplication to find that x=24,750,000/3, or 8,250,000 cm.

There were many times I wanted to quit. "I can't" was a refrain I had to beat out of my thoughts. Studying for the test was much more difficult and much less exciting than surfing or skiing. I thought about calling West Point back and asking if I could get a master's degree in literature or history, something requiring a few less numbers and mind's eye calculations. But even that would have required a Graduate Record Exam (GRE). The test preparation struck at the heart of my insecurities. I had conquered some physical challenges since losing my sight, but this was an intellectual task.

Blindness had altered more than just my ability to see. I often lost track of time—minutes and hours, even days and weeks. I could remember events, but something about the lack of sight made it difficult for me to put those events in chronological order. All of my memories were now auditory. In the short term, that made multiple-choice questions incredibly difficult.

Tiffany and I pressed on, one question at a time. I'm guessing the idea of giving up tempted Tiff just as it did me. The practice could be incredibly frustrating for her. But God had provided a glimpse of what He might have in store for us, and we worked hard to keep each other going. We knew we could not give up. As always, Tiffany stood by me and provided exactly what I needed.

A few years earlier, Liz Riley, director of admissions at Duke's Fuqua School of Business, was sitting in a hotel room in South Africa when a familiar voice sounded on the television. An army major was explaining the dire circumstances surrounding the injury of two of his unit's soldiers. "Oh my gosh," chimed Liz, "that is Chip Daniels." The others in the room looked at her quizzically.

"He's a Fuqua alum!"

Lieutenant Colonel Chip Daniels and Lieutenant Colonel Everett Spain—who was an aide to General David Petraeus and later a White House Fellow—are just two of the Duke M.B.A.'s who built an enduring reputation of excellence for army-sponsored students during Liz Riley's tenure. "They just make me so proud," brags Liz. "They are just the greatest people."

The reputation of my predecessors bolstered my own application for admission. "Because of the track record with West Point, we knew you would be a great fit with our culture and would positively contribute to our community," Liz Riley said later. "We as a university just had to figure out if we could put together the resources you would need to be successful academically."

One of my admissions essays detailed my moment of desperation in the Palo Alto parking lot. It painted a picture of all I had been through and all I would hopefully bring to the table. That essay emboldened Liz and moved her further down the path to admitting me, but Fuqua had never had a blind student. Setting the precedent appeared attractive from one perspective but daunting from another. As Liz worked through the scenario with the university's Office of Student Disabilities, she received a letter from General Petraeus, who was commanding all ground forces in Iraq. Coach K., who rarely sent personal notes to the business school, also sent a letter. "Because he wrote a letter for you," Liz noted, "and followed up several times, we knew it was important to him. But we still had to make the right choice for the right reasons. If we didn't think you could handle the pace and the rigor, we would have told you that Duke was not the right place."

By the time the GMAC finally called and summoned me to a small test-taking center in Virginia, the second-round deadline at Duke had passed, but I had submitted the rest of my application, and the school had agreed to defer its decision until I had taken the GMAT. On test day, things only got more difficult. For months, Tiffany had been reading questions and answers to me. For the main event, the test center assigned me a reader, someone with whom I was completely unfamiliar. Worse yet, I was the first blind person to take the GMAT at this particular center, so the reader had no experience with sightless business school candidates. For eight hours, I took in words, visualized equations, and fed back answers. Oh my stars, a root canal would have been slightly more pleasant.

Fortunately, Duke was not pinning its belief in me on my test score. Explained Liz: "In this instance, we decided that the GMAT was not necessarily going to be the best indicator. Everything else we looked at said you could be successful." Liz Riley's head eventually reached the conclusion that her heart had drawn when she first heard my story: I would make it and I would hopefully bring value to Duke in some way. In March of 2007, Liz Riley called me and told me that I had been accepted into the M.B.A. program at Duke.

Chapter 23

OUR CALLING

There are only two ways to live your life. One is as though nothing is a miracle. The other is as though everything is a miracle.
Albert Einstein

Not long after Duke accepted me, Jeff Van called to say that the freshmen (or plebe) class at West Point wanted me to come back as a guest speaker. Every time I receive an offer to speak, I pray about it. Speaking is not something I like to do, but by the spring of 2007, it was becoming clear that God had a purpose for me that included sharing my story with others. Unlike most of my opportunities to speak, this invitation to West Point didn't really make me nervous. Sure, I would be talking to over a thousand people, but these people *chose* me. What I had to say was relevant to their lives and to their futures. My fear is more about whether people will accept me than whether I will trip over my words.

Even so, as I prepared to climb the stage and address the plebes, insecurities ran through my head. *Does my uniform look okay? Will the cadets think that I look funny? I have lots of badges on my uniform, but will they think less of me because I can't see?* After Cadet Bill Herbert detailed the circumstances of my injury, provided a brief background, and then introduced Jeff, the crowd sounded out some applause. I placed my arm on Jeff's elbow and climbed three stairs to the stage in West Point's Robinson Auditorium. Twelve hundred cadets and a number of others continued to clap and cheer as I stood awkwardly, facing the crowd. Having Jeff there with me eased the tension some. I knew he was a respected member of the faculty, and being associated with him made me feel a little more respected too.

Jeff tried to wait out the applause, but eventually gave up and joined in. I feigned a yawn to mask my embarrassment. Trying to comfort me, Jeff turned and whispered, "Way to go, Scoots." After a brief video, Major Van Antwerp (he'd been promoted) took the podium and talked about leadership. He provided themes that echo through his life: people, relationships, and fighting through adversity. "Our lives don't always work out according to our ideal scenario," said Jeff.

Jeff shared the story of Captain Bill Jacobsen and his death in the Mosul mess hall bombing. He asked the cadets to reflect on a widow and four children. He detailed how he took over Alpha Company in the wake of Bill's passing. Finally, he described for the cadets the intimate details of my injury. After acting out the hand motions of the driver in the gray Opel and climaxing with the explosion, Jeff quoted John 15:13: "Greater love has no one than this, that he lay down his life for his friends."

Major Van then played a video that Luke Van Antwerp had made about the realities and challenges surrounding my injury. With the song "You Are God Alone" blaring in Robinson Auditorium, the crowd watched scenes from my life. They saw Tiffany and me at Ranger School graduation. They saw me with Edward Graham, Dave Webb, and Adam Rivette. They saw me on a couch in a living room in DuPont, Washington, waving childishly at the camera. They saw me in Iraq, surrounded by kindergarten-aged children. And then the next thing they saw was me with three-quarters of a skull, lying in a hospital bed at Walter Reed. There was video of the Purple Heart ceremony, flashes of scenes from Iraq, and me coming face-to-face with my baby nephew Luke Smiley. I was caught in still frame with a medal on my chest, tears streaming down my face. The cadets saw the green Trojan helmet, Jeff giving me a haircut, and Tiffany holding my hand as I walked outside, as a blind man, for the first time. All the while, the song played. *In the good times and bad, you are God alone.* I was still holding on to that truth, every day. I was making the decision to get out of bed and smile, trusting God had a future for me.

After the video finished, I once again grabbed Jeff's arm and followed him up to the stage. Standing behind the podium, wearing my army combat uniform and my Combat Infantry Badge, Airborne wings, and scuba bubble, suggesting I was still proud of being a soldier, I told the crowd, "That video always gets me," as if I could see it. And in my mind I can, because I was there, in every one of those pictures.

Fighting back tears, although I had told the story numerous times before, I spoke of the man in the Opel. It was the last thing I ever saw. "I woke up ten days later, and the first thing I remember is my dad giving me a kiss good-bye, because he had been with me for over a week."

Although they probably thought I was crazy, I admitted that, for a while, I truly believed I would recover and head back to Iraq. My soldiers needed me. As I spoke, nobody made a sound. Chances were that several of these future officers would die in combat. Some would come home severely wounded, maybe even blind. They would struggle with their new lives; they would need a light in the darkness. I hoped what I had to say would be an encouragement to them in the future. Life goes on, and we can still triumph in the midst of adversity. I didn't brag about any of my successes—surfing or skiing or getting into Duke. But because of those successes, I found I believed in my own message. It was authentic. If we don't give up, we *can* live.

I told them the rest of the story. Surgery. Darkness. Paralysis. Desperation. Hospitals. Finality. Struggles. Recovery. Family. Friends. God. When I finished, Jeff came back up and humbled me with his graciousness. He talked about how I truly did care for my soldiers, and how I saw my injury as being more than just a personal struggle. It was about others as well. That was my sincere desire—through the struggle to keep serving others with love.

"You are going to be standing in front of a platoon before you know it," promised Jeff. "Use this time at West Point to get ready. Think about who you are. Think about when you are experiencing adversity, when you are a Scott Smiley and you have lost your eyesight and you can't move the right side of your body. Are you going to just sink inside and focus on yourself and say, 'To hell with everybody else—so what if I've got a five-year commitment to the army? So what if I have a wife who needs me and a family who cares about me? So what if I have soldiers back in Iraq, forty-four of them, who are wondering how I am doing and, just, living and dying by my slight improvements?'

"A selfish person," finished Jeff, "doesn't become a selfless leader."

Jeff's words were awesome, and I hoped in that moment that my efforts to drive on with life had provided some hope as well. The crowd clapped, and Jeff told me everyone was standing. When people applaud after I have spoken, I feel like I have accomplished something. I know it is not about me. Standing on the podium, I silently thanked God for the opportunity.

Jeff's words notwithstanding, it was Tiffany who was the star. During a question-and-answer session, a freshman cadet stood and fumbled his syllables into the microphone. "Sir, uh, actually both sirs, uh, can I ask your wives a question?"

The crowd murmured. There's always one cadet, every lecture, who asks *that* question. Everyone in the audience anticipated it was on its way. "Ladies, I was wondering, uh, what gives you the strength every day, with trying times, with knowing that your husbands go off to fight wars, to maybe not come back; what gives you the strength every day?" It was actually a good question.

"I can speak only for myself," said Tiffany, brushing past me to reach the microphone, "but I believed in what my husband was doing. He had trained. He believed in what he was doing—there was such purpose in what he was doing. I supported him . . . I mean it was hard when he left; we were both crying that day. We said good-bye, and you don't know what to expect. You don't know. But we both took it. This was our calling. He was serving his country, and that's an honor. Not everyone can say they do that. Or have done it."

Tiffany's momentum built as she continued: "A lot of Americans frankly, today, don't want to do that. They don't know what it means to sacrifice. That's probably part of our problem here in America." As the crowd interrupted Tiffany with applause that sounded like a frightening hailstorm, she apparently smiled bashfully.

"And going through the injury, it's something you never expect to happen—but obviously there was another path. The injury, the phone call, it was hard for Jeff and me. But I met Scotty at Walter Reed, and when they told me, 'Get ready for your husband's medical retirement,'

I was like, 'Nope, he's gonna serve,' and so he later made that decision himself.

"It is a dedication to what we sacrificed. And I still support all of these guys, and I support Scotty in all he does."

I was so proud of her.

My life had accelerated from zero to sixty in under four months. I'd gained admission to a great business school; I *really* was headed back to West Point to teach leadership; and Tiffany's stomach had expanded to the size of a large watermelon—she was eight months pregnant.

At a Fort Monroe function where senior officers exchange pleasantries, one where we felt typically out of place, Tiffany inched up to Paula Van Antwerp, Jeff's mom, and quietly announced that she was having contractions. "They are still ten minutes apart," whispered Tiff, "but if this is it, would you be able to drive me to the hospital?"

Tiffany's contractions stayed at ten minutes for much of the night. She took me on several walks, trying to kick-start her system into full-blown labor. We walked at midnight. We walked at two A.M. Then at five the baby got anxious. It was not my idea of a good night's sleep.

"Scotty, it's time."

Paula raced to the house to find us waiting by the front door. Mrs. Van escorted Tiffany to the car and guided her wobbly body into the front seat. She then came and got me, leading me to the back. A few minutes later, we were at the hospital at Langley Air Force Base. With the help of a nurse, Paula assisted Tiffany into a wheelchair, showed me the way to the waiting room, and then, once we were under the watchful eye of the hospital staff, wished us the best and headed home.

We were not allowed to check in at first. The nurse told us Tiffany was not quite ready, so we walked around the hospital for about forty-five minutes. We both had to endure the labor pains. I was tired and hungry and asked Tiffany if she could find me some food. We walked to the cafeteria in the hospital, where I sat down to eat a bagel with cream cheese and drink a cup of hot coffee.

Meanwhile, Tiffany was dealing with more painful contractions as I sat. The cook in the cafeteria came over and with fear in his voice asked if Tiffany was okay. I just looked up and said, "Yeah, she'll be fine," and got back to enjoying my bagel.

Just a few minutes later, I called Paula Van's cell phone. "Mrs. Van, we didn't bring a camera. Would you mind going back and getting us one? And, oh yeah, Tiffany was wondering if you would be her labor coach?"

Inside the delivery room, Tiffany, who had chosen to endure a natural childbirth, grunted and panted through the breaks in rapidly escalating contractions. I found myself focusing on Tiffany's noises—there was really nothing else for me to concentrate on. "Tiffany"—I smirked—"do you have to pant so loud? What's going on over there?" Had she not been preoccupied, Tiffany would have grabbed the telephone and thrown it at my head.

"Come on Tiffany. It can't be that bad. The noises are so out of control. You are all I can hear." At that moment, Tiffany wished I had been blind, deaf, and mute. I was not as funny as I thought I was. (Yes, I was.)

After only a few hours of labor, Tiffany flexed her birthing muscles and screamed out a brand-new Smiley. At crunch time, I kept my comments to myself. Although we hadn't had the camera and birth coach all that well planned (seeing that the baby came three weeks early), we *had* thought through the very moment of birth. Not even the doctor looked below the baby's waist. Standing at the foot of the bed, he secured our newborn in his grip and slotted the baby's groin into my cupped hands—much as a center would hike the ball to his quarterback. Sensing the presence of a tiny little penis, I announced to the room: "It's a boy!"

Tiffany swears that not an eye was dry. It was truly an awesome moment. Two years before, I had been living in a hospital room not unlike this one. I'd been lying there, unable to do much of anything for myself, wondering where my life was headed. Now, although I couldn't see with my own eyes God's miracle of childbirth, holding that baby in my hands was enough for me. With some help, to make sure the scissors were in the right place, I cut Grady's umbilical cord. After the nurses cleaned him, wrapped him in a blanket, and handed him to Tiffany, I snuggled up beside my wife and my new son. I wondered what I had done to be so blessed.

Chapter 24

MIXED EMOTIONS

From everyone who has been given much,
much will be demanded; and from the one who
has been entrusted with much, much more will be asked.
The gospel according to Luke (chapter 12, verse 48)

Less than two months after Grady was born, I made it to the top of Mount Rainier. The day that I made it up to the summit, I was supposed to have been in Washington, D.C., for the festivities surrounding my designation as the 2007 *Army Times* Soldier of the Year. Tiffany, with a two-month-old in her arms, had agreed to tackle the hobnobbing while I came down the mountain. Micah Clark, who had talked me into climbing Rainier, promised to get me to D.C. by the next day.

Once you are on top of Rainier, you are only halfway done with the trip. Micah had called in all of his contacts to explore the options for delivering me to the nation's capital. The most elaborate version involved a couple of F-18s taxiing me across the country at nearly twice the speed of sound. My blindness got in the way—the navy decided that if I was going to fly in the world's premier fighter jet, I had to be able to see.

Micah ended up settling for a helicopter ride to Sea-Tac Airport, where I jumped on a flight and flew to D.C. via standard passenger plane—all after four members of the climbing team had placed me in a toboggan and raced me down the hill. Although I felt kind of bad that all these other guys had to pull me down the mountain, I didn't feel *that* bad. I was smoked.

While I had been preparing to climb Rainier, one of my friends and his platoon of soldiers in Iraq happened upon an opportunity to capture a key terrorist. The man was the number two target on the U.S. Army's most wanted list, an operative who had commissioned tens, even hundreds, of suicide car bombers during the first four years of the war in Iraq. American forces had been on alert for days, ready to move out in an instant to bring this terrorist to justice. Credible reports suggested he would be in the vicinity of my friend during the next five days. Based on that information alone, an entire platoon (forty men) waited. And waited. And waited. Like hunters in a deer stand. On the fifth day of standby, about to go crazy from the constant tension between boredom and finger-on-the-trigger alertness, the unit received word from its higher headquarters: the terrorist was on his way.

The platoon rolled out the gates in minutes, moved to the decisive point of the operation, and secured a nondescript building in a small Iraqi shopping village. All exits were covered. With exacting precision, the world's best soldiers penetrated the safe house, busted down doors, and cleared rooms.

Nothing. He wasn't there.

My friend, directing the operation from a key vantage point across the street, told me that he was baffled. His men had the whole block secured. That building—that was where the terrorist was supposed to be. The small shopping center looked like a ghost town. Even a piece of tumbleweed couldn't have sneaked down a back alley.

Where did he go? wondered my buddy.

As the story goes, my friend spotted an aimless civilian walking down the center of the village's main road, coming right at him. At first he was confused, but he explained to me that his confusion quickly turned into gut instinct. *This doesn't look right,* he thought. *We have the whole village cordoned by soldiers with machine guns. Where did this guy come from?*

Momentarily distracted by the radio communications of one of his team members, my friend almost failed to notice that the aimless civilian, dressed in traditional Islamic clothing, had passed right in front of him. *No way!* A mental image of the terrorist, a face he had studied for weeks, locked in sync with the person he had just seen.

"Hey you, stop!" my buddy commanded in Arabic. He elevated his weapon to horizontal and took eight steps forward. He ordered the man to raise his hands and rotate 180 degrees. When the man's face had turned on the axis of his body, my fellow infantryman knew. It was him—Abu Shahid, the mastermind behind my blindness. One of my very best friends looked Abu Shahid in the eye and said: "Gotcha."

I wasn't entirely sure why I was Soldier of the Year. Other men and women were across the world, catching bad guys, providing safety for Iraqis, and missing their families. While I understood the gravity of my situation and the positive example demonstrated by my resolve, I knew that other people had problems much bigger than mine: mothers and fathers who had lost a son, kids growing up without anything to eat, soldiers who had lost not only their eyes but their mental capacity or their will to live. I was getting ready to start my master's in business administration, for goodness' sake. I considered myself immeasurably blessed. Not because of Duke but because of Grady. Not because I'd met Team USA and climbed Mount Rainier but because of Tiffany. Most of all, I now held in my heart the knowledge that God loved me and that He was in control. If I could not have handled blindness, then I believe God would not have allowed it. I was growing in trust.

But the celebration in D.C. was not just about me, or even about me. It was about a new way of looking at our wounded warriors. I was the first soldier blinded in combat to stay on active duty. My determination provided some inspiration while echoing similar triumphs of others.

I had mixed emotions about some of the blessings coming my way. Guys were carrying me down mountains and flying me in helicopters. I'd sat courtside while the NBA's best players scrimmaged. On the one hand, the attention was tough to receive. Blindness was now my life, and I struggled as I received recognition for making the choice to live. And yet, I had given my eyes in service of our country. I didn't feel like I deserved anything special, but to be honest, I didn't necessarily feel I should turn it all down. As my confidence grew, I wanted more than anything to help others. If my story could inspire, then I wanted it to inspire. I had needed Andrew Harris and General Van and my friends and family. Maybe somebody needed me.

Before a packed house on Capitol Hill, Representative Doc Hastings, who had appointed me to West Point back in 1999, presented me as the Soldier of the Year. I tried to emphasize what I felt about being a representative of many others in service. "I feel great,"

I said, "but I definitely think there are other soldiers who deserve this award. Lots of people have gone through trials and tribulations, have given so much. I am just one of them."

The next summer, I was blessed with another great experience. During the middle of 2008, ESPN made me one of five nominees for the Best Outdoor Athlete ESPY. Blind skiing, surfing, skydiving, and mountain climbing caught the attention of someone. I still have no idea who nominated me for the ESPY. I learned about the nomination from a friend who had been tuned in to ESPN. I thought the guy was messing with me until my brother Neal confirmed that he had seen the nomination online. It was amazing to be up for such an award, but as an athlete, I wasn't even in the same category as the other people.

The nomination earned Tiffany and me a trip to the Nokia Theatre in the heart of L.A.'s entertainment district. The 2008 gala boasted a guest list that included Kevin Garnett, Venus and Serena Williams, Will Ferrell, Eli Manning, Danica Patrick, Zac Efron, David and Victoria Beckham, Forest Whitaker, and host Justin Timberlake.

Nokia Theatre's blue and pink lights, its red carpet, and its flock of limousines were about as far away from Pasco, Washington, as Tiffany and I had ever been (Iraq included). We were in the middle of a truly unique culture. Surrounded by celebrity, we had an amazing opportunity to connect with icons, except that I could not see. Despite her athletic background, Tiffany hadn't spent much of her last few years reading *Sports Illustrated* or watching *SportsCenter*. She was clued in enough to know that we were standing behind some older NFL quarterback as we waited to enter the theater, but her sports knowledge flamed out right about there.

"Who is that?" I asked, nodding in the direction of a loud laugh.

"I'm not sure," Tiffany replied. I could see her, as I'd seen her before, scrunching her shoulders together, turtling her head down toward her heart, and clinching her teeth. "It's a tall African-American guy; he's probably close to seven feet."

"Well, is it Kevin Garnett or LeBron James?"

A group of laughing athletes walked by a few moments later. "Who was that? Who was that?" I fired out the question like a third-grader walking down Main Street in the Magic Kingdom. This was cool stuff.

"I'm not sure. These three really big guys," answered Tiffany.

There I was at the ESPYs and I couldn't even meet famous people because my wife didn't know who anyone was! I did get a chance to talk to North Carolina basketball player Tyler Hansbrough, but he didn't say much—just "kew" (Tar Heel for "cool," I guess) when I told him the brief version of my story.

I won the ESPY for Best Outdoor Athlete that night, but I didn't get the chance to offer my acceptance speech. My award was relegated to the post-show credits—the athletic equivalent of the "Cinematography in a Documentary Film" treatment. The ESPYs were not likely one of those events where people wanted to hear what I had to say, so I was kind of relieved that I didn't have to give a speech. I figured I wasn't in the same class as all of those other athletes and would have looked out of place. What I had been looking forward to, however, was the awesome chance to thank God in front of all those people. But for whatever reason, God did not need me to speak that evening, and I was fine with that.

Before we left, Tiffany pulled the older quarterback's name out of her memory and said it: Brett Favre. We were standing in line behind Brett Favre.

CHAPTER 25

ABOVE WATER

Do or do not. There is no try.
Yoda

Tiffany has moments when she feels like other people are against us. "I don't know why," she told me, "but there are just times when I feel like other people want you to fail, like they'd be happy if you were just a blind guy who couldn't do it." She can't explain where exactly the feeling comes from. She knows that it first hit her at Walter Reed, when the medical staff assumed away the rest of my military career. The feeling struck her again at Fort Lewis, when the medical evaluation boards geared back up. But after General Van Antwerp helped us through that process, Tiffany grew more comfortable with our situation. Until my first term at Duke, that is.

At first it was the little stuff—a woman in student services who suggested that my locker would be on the first floor even though the rest of my class would have lockers up above. "The stairs could get dangerous," she suggested. At another point, a staff person, whispering to Tiffany in a doubtful tone during one of my many trips to the bathroom (I drink a lot of water), said, "I don't know how he is going to do it. I just don't know."

Later it was big stuff—like me trying to pass my classes. I endured the first two weeks of probability and statistics without any assistance. I just sat there, in the back of a lecture hall full of stadium seating, listening to people talk about equations and Excel spreadsheets. My accounting professor would say, "You just take this and move it here. Move this so that, and see, you have the answer." *No, I don't see.* At certain moments, I started to feel sick to my stomach, wondering how I was going to get through this and wondering why God had brought me to this place only to see me fail.

Eventually, Duke provided me second-year students to help with each of my classes, but as the term went on, that volunteer tutor system broke down. The students assigned to help me had other demands on their time, like finishing their own M.B.A.'s and finding jobs in a declining economy. I felt like a burden. Even when the peer tutors were available for help, the friction of having five different people helping me with five different classes wore on my brain. I was making it—even doing better than average in most of my classes—but the pace at which I was running was quickly breaking me down.

Once again, I was on the precipice of *I can't,* feeling desperate and communicating my hopelessness to God. "Lord, if there is a reason you don't want me to succeed, then okay. I'll deal with it, and I'll explain it to the army later." I pressed on. I gave it everything I had. Tiffany and I would sit at our dinner table and enter formulas into Excel. I'd tell her where numbers were supposed to go, and she would put them there. It was like taking one step at a time up Mount Rainier. I didn't think I could keep going, but I did.

Heading into finals, I felt like I was hurtling toward a waterfall. I e-mailed the dean of students: "If we don't figure out something different—some other form of assistance—I think I am going to drown."

The dean seemed stumped as to how the situation had devolved. Some finger-pointing ensued, and then Tiffany's world started to crumble.

Tiffany's frustration was partly due to her concern about me failing out of Duke, but it was also about something else: a lack of community. She felt like she knew no one. She felt isolated, as if no one was on our team. The cords that had held Tiffany's world together during the previous two years had not only unraveled, they had vanished. Up until the journey to Duke, she'd had family and friends at every stop. She'd even had the structure of the army, warts and all, to hold her up. When I took off my uniform and Tiffany, Grady, and I moved into a town home on the south side of Durham, North Carolina, Tiffany was alone, really, for the first time in her life. Her mom was not there; her sisters, Michelle and Nicole, were not there; Therese Van Antwerp and Tanya Webb weren't there. It was just Tiffany and me and our three-month-old baby.

That first term at Duke was brutal on Tiff. The human side of her wanted to crush some people. Later, though, she was able to identify redeeming value in that time. "It just taught me again that the Lord takes care of you," she told me.

Care came in the form of a woman named Meena Dorr, a mother of three and a graduate of the University of Chicago's M.B.A. program. Meena's complexion gives away her Indian heritage, but her demeanor and country twang seem like a cross between Jersey Shore and Texas Panhandle. The day before Liz Riley caught word of my struggles to stay afloat and of some of the internal complications in getting me assistance, she had hired Meena to serve as a part-time applications reader in Duke's M.B.A. admissions office. The next day, Liz called her new employee and offered her a different job.

Meena had not been in school for fifteen years. She had to study on her own in order to help me study. She went to all of my classes with me (during our first term together). With an affectionate laugh, Meena admits that she treated me like her child, but we built a great rapport. Meena was exactly what I needed. She believed in me, she was committed to me, and most important, she was one person with one tutoring style. I needed someone who knew what I had studied and what I had already covered—one individual to whom I could always turn without feeling like I was a burden. I did not want to be a burden.

In class, especially in those involving long equations or graphs, Meena would explain to me what the professor was doing and why he or she was doing it. Meena didn't do the analysis or draw the conclusions, but she helped me structure things in a way that made the material digestible for a blind person. Blindness to me was still new. I didn't know exactly what I needed. Meena provided a consistency that made my experience so much more efficient. Tiffany and I were incredibly grateful. Meanwhile, Meena developed a close friendship with our entire family, even traveling to Pasco. Ours is a tight-knit relationship that lasts to this day.

The first year of an M.B.A. program is typically rigorous, time-consuming, and focused on the fundamental disciplines of business and management. With Meena at my side, my feet weren't kicking so hard underneath the water, and I finished out the final two terms with solid grades and no further issues. God had definitely provided—and just in time. During my second year, I had the opportunity to enjoy the Duke experience a bit more.

In September, the athletic department asked me to flip the coin at the beginning of the Duke-Navy football game. I met the athletic director on the sidelines before marching out to the fifty-yard line on a beautifully sunny day in Durham. The captains from each team shook hands, the referee handed me something metal and circular, and then I tossed it into the air. After my launching of the ceremonial coin, I heard a player on my left announce: "Heads."

"It is heads," said the ref as I replayed in my mind the many times I had performed this same ritual during my senior year in high school.

"Navy has won the toss."

The Navy midshipmen elected to defer their selection to the second half. On hearing this news, the Duke captain declared, "We will kick." *What?* I was confused. Why would Duke forgo possession? It didn't make sense. Out of nowhere, I felt emboldened. *Should I say something?* There was no way I was going to let Navy football gain any unnecessary advantages.

"Excuse me," I interrupted before the ref could respond to the Duke selection, "but you don't want to do that."

"Huh?" said one of the Duke players, probably wondering what this blind army guy was talking about. *Aren't you just here to flip a coin?*

"You don't want to do that," I said again. "You don't want to go back and tell your coach that Navy won the toss, elected to defer, and you decided to kick. Because then they'll get the ball this half *and* next half." Thousands of fans were probably wondering what the guys at the center of the field were discussing.

"Oh," murmured the Duke captain. "Oh, well, uh, I guess we will receive."

The Navy and Duke players shook hands again, turned, and jogged back to their respective benches. I had just earned our football team an extra possession, even if no one else knew it at the time. More important, I had just been a bit more me. Had I been able to see, I would have had no problem correcting the Duke players (of course, I never would have been out there tossing the coin in the first place). But as a blind guy, I felt a bit unsure of myself, like it wasn't my place to say anything, or like I might not fully grasp what was happening. That moment restored a bit of my confidence. Blind or not, I knew football.

"Good call," said the ref as I turned with my escort (my brother Neal) to walk off the field. "Good call."

I hadn't been a huge basketball fan in high school or at West Point, but at Duke I had a great opportunity to enjoy the sport, multiple chances to sit right behind the Duke bench at the invitation of Coach K.

On a Sunday night in February, I passed through the foyer doors in Cameron Indoor Stadium just a minute or so before game time. The stadium was hot, loud, and humid. To get to seat 65 in Row B, we would either have to pass right in front of the Duke bench, which would have taken about ten seconds, or walk the plank of the first row of bleachers in between two rows of standing fans. Another usher wouldn't let us out on the floor, so a friend helped me step up onto the bleacher that constituted Row B. I placed one foot in front of the other as my buddy held my elbow from behind and started out on what constituted about a fifty-foot journey.

Halfway through the trek, the stadium announcer called the crowd to its feet for the singing of the National Anthem. Now elevated about two feet above anyone around us, I took off my hat and placed my hand on my heart. At about "dawn's early light" I began to feel incredibly self-conscious. I wondered whose nose was trying to avoid a literal interaction with my butt cheeks. I imagined that the people across the court, a bunch of undergraduates known to the world as "Cameron Crazies," were looking at me, wondering why I was up so high. *Am I even facing the flag?*

At the sound of the word "brave," I let out a deep breath. This was the tension of my new life: because of my injury I had this opportunity to sit courtside, but my blindness could also make me feel helpless and self-conscious.

We navigated the last twenty-five feet and sat down right behind the Duke bench. From what people told me, Coach Krzyzewski was unusually rowdy at the outset of the game, rallying his players with arm waves, shouts, and pats on the backs—looking more cheerleader than coach. As Coach K. fired up players in the pregame huddle, I slipped a small headphone into my right ear and flipped on a radio. From the left side, I took in the sounds around me: players calling out screens, whistles, buzzers, students, and Coach K. From the right side I received play-by-play from a radio announcer who was sitting just fifteen feet away.

Duke fell behind early, but a heroic effort from junior Gerald Henderson kept the Blue Devils in arm's reach of Wake. Players shuffled up and down the court, battled for rebounds, and dove for loose balls just a few yards in front of me. I attempted to sync the sounds of the court with the sounds of the radio broadcast to piece together a complete game. At one point, Jon Scheyer faked a Wake defender into the air, and then took a three-pointer simply because he knew he was going to get fouled. Scheyer could have tossed me his jersey from the location of his jump shot—just a few feet out in front of the Duke bench. I could hear his feet hit the floor as the whistle blew, indicating a foul.

Minutes later, the heat and humidity of Duke's tiny gym forced Coach K. to strip off his suit coat. He tossed the blue jacket behind him like it was a soiled towel. The jacket landed in my lap.

In the end, Duke pulled out a ten-point victory. Heading down the hill from the stadium after the game, I heard a golf cart speed by and turn a corner a little too sharply. The golf cart bottomed out, and when I caught the sound of metal meeting concrete, I turned to my friend and asked: "Whoa, how many people do they have in that thing?" He was surprised by my ability to decipher the sounds of an overstuffed electric cart, but I have to compensate for my inability to see—my other senses are highly attuned. These kinds of trade-offs are just part of life.

At lunch the next day, it took me fifteen stabs to find a piece of lettuce with the tongs of my fork. Lettuce doesn't weigh a whole lot. It's not like a piece of meat or a small red potato. If you can't feel it, it's tough to get it onto the utensil. Truth is, I rarely have any idea what is going into my mouth, and I've had to learn not to care. I eat mostly to nourish my body because I've grown weary of expecting some steak and being surprised by broccoli.

Back at the Palo Alto facility, I once asked the lady with the crazy hat what was on my plate. She first told me that it was a hamburger. Then she stopped herself and changed her assessment to meat loaf. A few seconds later, she decided that it was apple sauce. My appetite disappeared right about the time she said "sauce."

Daily life has its difficulties. I can survive without being able to see a basketball game. What hurts beyond measure is not being able to see the people that I love—never being able to see Tiffany again. I feel her face. I feel her hair. I picture what she looks like, but I start to forget. People are always telling me how beautiful my son, Grady, is. Sometimes I even get jealous when others see my kids for the first time and get to rejoice in that. It's hard on me. It hurts so much that I try not to go there. I used to try and feel Grady's face, touch his nose. But every time I tried, he yelled, "Tissue!" I simply cannot picture what he looks like, and descriptions just don't do any good. "He has blond hair. He has beautiful eyes. He looks a lot like you." Nothing. I can't see him.

This is one of my losses. It hurts, but my hope is in the Lord. Every day I must choose to embrace the life He gave me. The first thing I will see when I get to heaven is Christ's face. That gets me through the hard times.

CHAPTER 26

EVERY DAY

For I consider that the sufferings of this present time are not worthy to be compared with the glory that is to be revealed to us.
The apostle Paul, in his letter to the Romans (chapter 8, verse 18)

Jeff Van Antwerp said he sometimes looks at me and wonders, "What is he thinking about right now? What is it like to not be able to see?" When it was my turn to carry Grady down the five wooden steps that led from the back door of our Durham town home to our one-car garage, I was thinking: *If I miss a stair I am going to crush my little boy.* Although my life with Grady in Durham teemed with moments when I hoped not to trip, spill, or bump into something, I did my absolute best to be a great dad. On the occasions when I did miscalculate the angle to make it through a doorway and bumped into a wall, I would tell Grady, "Watch where you're going."

The first time I took care of Grady by myself I was a little nervous that I would lose him or something, but it worked out okay. Okay except for the diaper change. Unable to see, I had to feel around to figure out what I was doing. I thought Grady had just peed, but when my hands started working through a claylike substance, I realized Grady had delivered me a squishy brown present. We were both a mess. The poop was all over my hands and all over Grady. I had to find the bathtub and wash him off. I had to find his clothes and evacuate them to the washer. The whole house started to smell like a Port-a-Potty.

It was Liz Riley's job to admit a cohort of Duke M.B.A.'s who brought with them diverse experiences so that the members of the class learned as much from one another as they did from their professors. I did my best to carry my own academic load. I admit that I struggled in accounting, but that is why I had teammates like Kohei, Happy, David, and Echo alongside me—they picked me up when I was down.

In terms of life experience, I hope I brought a lot to the program. Bipa, another one of my teammates, encouraged me, reminding me often about the unique role I played as a blind father. To my astonishment, Bipa and the rest of the class of 2009 selected me to be student speaker for Fuqua's mid-May graduation ceremony. I never saw that coming. I made it through the M.B.A. program and did well, but I didn't graduate at the top of my class. I was stunned the other students picked me to talk. I was also terrified. This would be a speech, not a talk. I couldn't get up there and just tell my story. I had to memorize something. What would I do if I lost my place?

The day before graduation I sat down with Coach K. for a farewell and a pep talk. I told Coach about the time I shared my story at North Shore Christian Fellowship. "I just cried for a long time and didn't say anything intelligent."

Coach K. listened. When I had finished, he sat forward and issued a direct order: "Don't you be humble about this. I'm serious. You had a huge moment, a fork in the road. I don't know if I would have done what you did, and what you did is going to have a big impact. It's going to motivate people to do good. I'm serious, Smiley. Your life is going to ripple through a lot of people. Your decisions and the way you live. The guys on the Olympic team noticed Tiffany and you; they noticed that you don't stay inward. The two of you have acted as one. They have moments—at the free throw line or with a few minutes left. Your moment was about life."

Coach's words impacted my heart. I fear coming across as special when I believe I am just blessed by God. I fear my words say, "Look at me," when really I'm just trying to give people hope. It helped to hear Coach tell me it was okay to bring some attention to myself for a higher purpose. Lots of people give speeches and write books. As long as God blesses me with these opportunities, and as long as people want to hear what I have to say, then I will share. When God calls me to do something else, I will do that.

Nick, my youngest brother, would have loved to come along to meet Coach K. in the penthouse room of the Duke athletics building, but Nick was asleep on the couch when I left for the meeting. He'd picked up a case of pink eye from Grady and was trying to sleep it off. Our entire family—minus my sister Kathleen and her husband, who were back in Pasco, and Stephen, who was out of the country—gathered for graduation. Even Colonel Kevin McDonnell had come down from Washington, D.C. In all, there were close to thirty people stuffed inside our town home, including a couple of Grady's cousins, his great-grandparents, and his aunt Shelly (Tiffany's sister). Grady, just a week shy of two, also had a sibling on the way. Tiffany was seven months pregnant.

Friday night, as it had been for the last couple of decades with our family, was pizza night. The night before graduation, our time together was a good reminder that even though my eyesight was gone, the love of my family was constant.

What I wanted to tell my classmates at our graduation was that this is a brief life. That we are here on earth for just a short time. That our eternal perspective is what matters. I wanted to tell them about the depth of my despair at Walter Reed—how taking a shower had been a major victory; how a friend named Andrew Harris had given me a spark that allowed me to believe in myself. I wanted to tell them about the Palo Alto parking lot and the moment I realized I was completely dependent on God, when I saw that life wasn't about what I could rack up in my own accomplishments but about trusting in Him. I wanted to tell them that even with my hope set on an eternal reward, life is still tough and requires grit and perseverance, and that if I could do it with no eyes, then they could do it too. I wanted to share how it hurt not to be able to see my wife and child, but how I carried the hope that someday I will see them—in heaven—and it will be amazing.

I wanted to say that in so many ways, I am a needy, dependent man now that I am blind but that, as singer Jeremy Camp puts it, "This life is not the finish line." And I can't not choose God. I've been angry and depressed. I've doubted and searched. But God picked me up, and He continues to guide me one step at a time. My endurance and accomplishments are partly the result of who I am, but mostly the result of what I believe—of *who* I believe. I would not share with my classmates all that was on my heart, but my hope was to encourage them.

On Saturday morning, I walked onto the playing floor of Cameron Indoor Stadium, wearing a standard black graduation gown, one of those square hats, and holding the arm of a classmate as I navigated the center aisle. Up in the stands, Tiffany had on a green maternity dress. Sitting on her lap was a blond-haired, blue-eyed Grady in a light blue (Carolina blue) shirt and kid-sized Chuck Taylors. Bagpipes were playing.

My parents and grandparents had the privilege of sitting in folding chairs on the gym floor, just about ten rows to the left and twenty rows back from me; I was in the first row facing the stage on the right side. As the ceremony began, Lieutenant General and Paula Van Antwerp walked in from the back side of the gym and stood behind the cluster of folded chairs. Therese Van Antwerp (Jeff's wife) and her kids were there with Paula and Van, along with Jane Graham (Edward's mom) and several other friends.

After some standard graduation stuff, the class president introduced me with a short version of my story. "Please help me welcome our designated class speaker, Scotty Smiley," he announced. I followed the arm of a classmate to the podium and searched my brain. At Ranger School, I couldn't even get five stanzas of the creed out. Now I had to deliver an entire speech. I prayed I would make it through.

"When Diana Tyler let me know that I was chosen by you all, I was definitely humbled but kind of scared. I didn't know why I was picked. I thought maybe this was like *American Idol*, and if it was, you obviously haven't heard me or my wife sing . . . I finally concluded that it's because I'm so good looking." Everyone laughed, which led me to believe things were going okay. My nerves calmed a bit.

"Yes, so good looking. And I came to this conclusion because every time we'd bring my little boy Grady to school, all the girls in the class would say, 'Oh, how cute; he's so handsome.' And then they'd look up at me and say, 'He looks just like you.' So I want to thank you ladies for choosing me, and I guess all you guys who thought the same thing."

There was some applause mixed with laughter. When the crowd noise ebbed, I spoke of the suicide bomber, the blindness, and questioning God. I told the audience that I'd been willing to give my life. But my eyesight? I had a choice—to be like Lieutenant Dan in *Forrest Gump* or to reach down, stand up, and live a life of meaning. Then I shared some of the things I had reflected on when I considered getting to this point.

"I'm a Christian, and a verse that always has stayed true to me is *I can do all things through Christ who strengthens me.*" I waited out some more applause, and then I continued. "I questioned God. Did that still apply to me? Is my life still the same? And I finally concluded, yes it did, and I fought back. But it wasn't just because of my hard work or my desire. It was because of my wife's support. It was my family and my friends. It was the people who surrounded me and lifted me up."

I explained that as I recovered, I had the opportunity to come to Duke, semijoking that my trials hadn't ended when I was blinded. "I had to attend Luca's statistics class. And financial accounting class? I'm still not sure what an income statement is and what it has to do with cash flows." (From what I heard afterward, the blood rushed from the faces of a few faculty members and the crowd considered whether to laugh at this statement or cry.)

"I'm kidding. I do know what those things are, but it was you all who helped me with the story problems and helped me prepare for tests. I even needed help finding the restrooms—whether it was the men's or women's, I'm not sure it mattered."

On the day I received my Purple Heart, when General Van Antwerp told us that life was going to be great and it was going to be exciting, I never would have believed that I'd be standing up on a podium like this as the commencement speaker at Duke's business school. During the Purple Heart ceremony, I'd been lying in a hospital bed with one eye gone and the other worthless. My life seemed purposeless. God seemed distant. But since that time, I'd surfed, skied, skydived, welcomed a wonderful boy into the world (with another on the way), had an incredible wife standing shoulder to shoulder with me, and was still surrounded by a loving family and amazing friends. Most of all, my relationship with God was more meaningful than ever before. I finally felt worthy of being called an "Oak." My faith had been tested and it had survived, grown deeper. I hope my story will inspire people to live in a godly way, to trust and live in the light of something bigger than themselves. That was my hope at Duke as I got up and delivered that speech from memory (and I did remember the whole thing), even as it is still my hope today.

I thank God every day for the life I have been given.

CHAPTER 27

JOURNEY LINE

One of the most reliable indicators and predictors of true leadership is an individual's ability to find meaning in negative events and to learn from even the most trying of circumstances.
Warren Bennis and Robert J. Thomas, in "Crucibles of Leadership"

After the Duke graduation ceremony, we packed up our town home and drove north (with help from Tiffany's sister Michelle this time). A few days later, we arrived at West Point, our new home. We spent a few weeks in a hotel, and then in early June we moved into a three-bedroom house on Winans Road—a child-filled stretch of street at the United States Military Academy. Legend has it that so many kids once lived in the area that the superintendent told the faculty not to go near the neighborhood unless absolutely necessary. Eventually, the area took on the nickname Sesame Street. In mid-June we contributed to the madness. Our second son, Graham Elliott Smiley, was born just a few weeks after we settled in. Days later, I would begin my practice teaching in preparation for my new role as an instructor.

Winans Road is ideal for our family. There are speed bumps for safety. We have a small fenced-in yard, and there is a nice little park for Grady directly across the street. By the time we moved to West

Point, my older son had picked up on the idea that I wasn't quite like everyone else. He didn't stand at my feet silently when he wanted me to pick him up. He knew that he had to make some noise. When Grady and I go to the park together, Grady leads, pulling me along by the hand and directing us to the teeter-totter.

Grady's understanding of me works in his favor at times—he can get away with things even when I am looking. But sometimes it backfires. One night after dinner, Grady wanted to feed his recent addiction to *The Jungle Book*. He approached me at the kitchen table, placed his hand on my leg, and asked: "Bear Sessities, Da-da. Want Bear Sessities."

"Did Mom say it's okay?"

From what a friend told me later, Grady stared at the ground for an instant, rolled his blue eyes to the top right corners of his eye sockets, and declared, "Yep. Momma said yes."

"Are you sure?" I asked. I was skeptical, but I couldn't see his facial expressions.

"Yep. Yep."

Grady's lies spread out thicker than the contents of his diapers. Anyone who actually could see his body language would've known he hadn't even asked his mom. But I could not see him, and Grady had manipulated his voice to convey sincerity.

"Okay, Grady, I'm going to ask Mom."

By that time, the taste of the Bear Sessities song was so sweet in Grady's ears that he had talked himself into his own story. "Okay, Da-da. Okay."

Three minutes later Grady was in his room on his bed—his lies exposed by Tiffany, who had explicitly told him, "No more *Jungle Book* tonight."

Despite Grady's occasional attempts to pull the wool over my eyes, so to speak, he also treats me like a hero, his hero. While I was never sure I wanted to be the *Army Times* Soldier of the Year, I absolutely want to be Dad of the Year. When I get home from work, Grady will run to the door and jump into my arms. Twenty minutes later, we will be wrestling in the backyard. At night, I will "read" him stories and he'll ask me to do it again. Having that feeling of being a loving father is pure joy, something God has given me despite the things that were taken away.

As great as fatherly heroism feels, it wasn't necessarily going to help me in the classroom. Cadets at West Point are respectful. But standing in front of fifteen of them and delivering leadership content can still be traumatizing. Cadets' voices might not indicate you are boring them and wasting their time, but their faces will—mine did when I was a cadet. If you haven't planned a solid lesson, the guy in the corner will be fighting to keep his eyelids up. My problem was that I wouldn't be able to see their faces. I had to be ready to inspire every time I walked into the classroom.

Certainly cadets would be interested in my story, but the semester would be forty lessons long. I was going to have to learn how to teach and teach well. Being onstage for a group of college students can make the most confident of leaders temporarily insecure. My insecurity came out a bit as I thought about what I'd look like in front of the group. But that is why those of us new to the faculty practiced during the summer—to shake all that stuff out.

I signed up to teach my first practice class on the topic of transformational leadership. The concept is pretty straightforward. Leaders can use punishments and rewards to motivate temporary behavior. This is called "transactional" leadership. But leaders can do more; they can transform the values and beliefs of others for the long term. Leaders who do this demonstrate certain characteristics and behaviors, and those qualities are what we would be examining in the practice class. Transformational leaders—people like Martin Luther King Jr., Coach Herman Boone from *Remember the Titans,* or your favorite high school teacher—use unconventional strategies, care about individuals, demonstrate self-sacrifice, and communicate confidence. They inspire people to do more than expected.

I crafted a lesson plan that included stories about Jeff Van Antwerp—a transformational leader in my own life. I also prepared snapshot pictures of William Wallace from *Braveheart* and Michael Scott from *The Office.* I prepared a set of open-ended questions, designed to generate discussion: *In what way was William Wallace a transformational leader? How about Michael Scott? He tries; why does he fail?*

I could no longer see the classrooms on the third floor of Thayer Hall, but I had spent four years in rooms just like these. I knew what my classroom would look like. A window on the far side of the room looked out on the Hudson River. Twenty sterile-looking desks formed a U-shape around the square space, about three feet in from the side and back walls. Chalkboards covered the painted cement-block walls, and a 1980s-era television was perched in the right-front corner of the room. Above the window to the Hudson was a large analog clock. I would have to trust my students to keep track of the time.

A Dell desktop computer was stored in a tall wooden cabinet just underneath the television. My fellow instructors, who were role-playing cadets for training purposes, would be surprised when the robotic sound of the Jaws program read PowerPoint slides over the classroom speakers. But they would get used to it.

Minutes before the class was about to begin, as several majors, a couple of civilian professors, and a couple of colonels entered the classroom, I announced that I hadn't been hungry all day: "I'm too nervous." An experienced instructor followed my proclamation with the news that "the Supe's coming to your class." It was apparently a coincidence, but Lieutenant General Hagenbeck, the senior officer in charge of everything about the United States Military Academy, had decided to drop in on the first fifteen minutes of my first-ever class. The presence of Hagenbeck, a combat veteran who had commanded the 10th Mountain Division during Afghanistan's Operation Anaconda (the first major battle of the global war on terror), jolted my nerves. My hands weren't shaking yet, but my brain was.

For the first five minutes of class, my tongue shook without much control. I just had gobbledygook coming out of my mouth. I was talking to myself in my head while I was talking out loud: *What am I even saying?* Eventually I settled down and things seemed to go smoothly. Our department head and a civilian professor got in an argument about theoretical stuff that I didn't really understand yet (I'm assuming they had stepped out of the cadet role-playing mode), but it was a decent class. Colonel Bernie Banks, a former attack helicopter squadron commander, a Harvard graduate, and a cadet favorite, told me, "Well done." But Colonel Banks was always gracious. I knew I had a lot to learn about teaching.

With the initial belly flop into teaching out of the way, I dedicated myself to preparing my first ten lesson plans, an effort slowed by

Microsoft's "upgrade" from Office 2003 to Office 2007. At Duke, I had committed almost all the PowerPoint shortcuts to memory. Through the combination of different QWERTY keys, I knew how to underline words, copy and import slides, create new text boxes, and center headlines on the page. I could do about anything that anyone else could do. Office 2007 ruined all of that. With the introduction of its new menus and features, I was completely lost. The space bar just kept "dinging" as my cursor ran into a brick wall. For hours I would sit in my Thayer Hall office, with the light off, and play with key combinations in an effort to learn the new software. When my teaching mates passed by, they would flip on my light it for no other reason than it freaked them out to see me living like a bat.

One of the most powerful lessons in the West Point leadership curriculum asks cadets to construct a "journey line." The exercise requires each individual to chart his or her life experiences on a makeshift graph with an x-axis representing time and a y-axis that registers emotional energy (highs and lows). I crafted a journey line with Tiffany, Grady, and Graham at the peaks. My West Point graduation, Ranger School graduation, and high school state championship were just a few levels down. My valleys included moving to Pasco from Boise in fifth grade, the death of Captain Bill Jacobsen, and the explosion of the gray Opel. I provided a twist to my chart by inserting an enormous black rectangle that covered up everything to the right of my injury. I then advanced to the next slide, where the rest of my life came up in gray, signifying that things for me are different. It's a whole new world.

Leadership instructors at West Point share their journeys for many reasons: to teach, to open their lives up to cadets, to build trust, and to model a process of reflection and self-discovery that is central to leader growth. I had noticeable self-doubt heading into the first week of classes, but I hoped my life experience would offer learning to cadets that would take them beyond the books.

In addition to teaching preparation, I tried to do other things to reorient myself to the army, to fit in as just another captain at West Point. Each morning I went to CrossFit (an intense morning workout session that was sometimes attended by more than one hundred cadets). I would wake up at 0530 and hitch a ride down to a field that runs parallel to the Hudson River. By the river, I pounded out pull-ups and squats next to true fitness maniacs. One morning I participated in a routine called "Murphy." In tandem with a partner, we knocked out a mile run, three hundred squats, two hundred pushups, one hundred pull-ups, and then ran a half mile backward.

When Tiffany found my physical training shirt on the washer later that morning, she thought the CrossFit workout had involved some sort of swim. The morning had just been really, really humid. I loved being back in the groove of working out, leading, and interacting with leaders. Having a soaking-wet physical fitness uniform was great. Contributing to the army was great. I thanked God for everything he had provided.

One day, as I readied some teaching material in my Thayer Hall office, a colleague stepped in and asked me how many sections of leadership I wanted to teach that first semester.

I wasn't sure, so I asked, "How many does everyone else teach?"

"Four," he said.

"Then that's how many I want to teach."

Chapter 28

A Story

Teaching is a daily exercise in vulnerability.
Parker Palmer, *The Courage to Teach*

On a humid day in mid-August of 2009, I stood in front of a classroom full of seventeen West Point juniors, not able to see the looks on their faces. Just six years earlier, I had been a cadet—hanging out with Edward, Dave, and Adam, studying leadership, and preparing for war. My wife was then my girlfriend, I had hardly considered fatherhood, and both of my eyes worked fine. Now, I was the teacher. I was nervous and excited at the same time.

"Hi, I'm Captain Smiley. I'm blind. I can't see a thing."

And I have a story to share . . .

AFTERWORD

To read more about Scotty's first day in class at West Point (from the summer of 2009) or about the God-driven series of events that led to the writing of this book, visit us at BlueRudder.net.

ACKNOWLEDGMENTS

God has blessed me. I love Him and I thank Him. Everything I have is because of Him. This book is for His glory and not my own. I hope that shined through. Thank you, Lord, for all You have provided.

One of those blessings is an incredible network of family and friends, so many people that I can't even begin to name them all. So I will simply thank the woman who has stood by me and supported me every step of the way. Tiffany Smiley is an incredible woman. I love you with all of my heart and cherish all you have done for me.

My mom and dad, Neal and Carrie, Steven, Mary Lynn, Krista, Kathleen and Erik, and Nick have all been such huge supporters of me and of this process. So have all of the Elliotts—Doug and Karen (Mom and Dad 2), Travis and Julie, Michelle, and Nicole. With a special thanks to Nicole, who was there to help with Graham's birth as I attended meetings in New York.

I love all of you and thank you for every ounce of support.

As Doug and I wrote this book, many key people provided us guidance, assistance, and support. Our agent, Kathy Helmers of Creative Trust, worked through so many things with us. She was always gracious, kind, and optimistic—clearly God placed her in this process with full knowledge of what we would need to get us through. Thanks to everyone else at Creative Trust who helped out with logistics, including Meredith Smith and Jeanie Kaserman.

Those at Howard Books—Jonathan Merkh, Jennifer Willingham, Susan Wilson, and Becky Nesbitt—truly got behind this story. We thank you for believing in it and supporting it. Most important, we were blessed with two amazing editors—Cindy Lambert and Stacy Mattingly—who took our manuscript and helped us make it so much better. You were gracious and supportive as you provided tough but insightful feedback. We thank God for your contributions. The message of this story is so much stronger because of you.

We had help and support in so many ways. Thanks to Larry Olson for introducing us to Kathy. Thank you to Dave and Tanya Webb, Everett and Julia Spain, Scott and Miki Bridgman, Liz Riley, Coach Mike Krzyzewski, Van and Paula Van Antwerp, and Jeff and Therese Van Antwerp for welcoming us, feeding us, or even housing us as we conducted interviews. Thanks to Al Chase, Nicki Denman, Jessica Tucker, Anthony Bush, Scott Snook, and Dave Webb for initial reviews of our manuscript. You set us on the right course before we even had a publisher. Thanks as well to Mike Branham for late help with the explosion scene and to Jeff Richards for his genius idea on how to end the book. And thanks to the wonderful people who have supported hope launch: Rich Ward, John Inman, Bob Tippett, Kirt Shaffer, Robin Craven, Theresa Richardson, and Bryan Dunfee.

We also thank Amanda Miller, who took pictures of my first day of class as well as family pictures to be used in the book. Thanks to Tanya Webb, Kristy Graham, Therese Van Antwerp, and others for photos of past events. Thanks also to Gabe Rogel for letting use photos from Mount Rainier, Peter King for the surfing pictures, and Michael Perry for letting us use a quote from his article. Finally, thanks to Stephanie Kingston for her last-minute photography heroics.

A special thanks to Stephanie Crandall for allowing your husband to leave his job and write this book. Your support of him and your trust in the Lord is awesome. Thanks also to John, Jason, Mackenzie, and Timmy, who gave up television, movies, and eating out. And to Grady and Graham, for being the best boys ever and enjoying the ride with us. Thanks also to Michael Scott of Dunder-Mifflin, who has inspired me as a leader every day. (Just seeing if anyone made it this far.)